THE DEAD SEA SCROLLS
AND MODERN TRANSLATIONS
OF THE OLD TESTAMENT

The
DEAD SEA SCROLLS
& Modern Translations
of the Old Testament

HAROLD SCANLIN

Tyndale House Publishers, Inc.

WHEATON, ILLINOIS

Library of Congress Cataloging-in-Publication Data

Scanlin, Harold P.
  The Dead Sea scrolls and modern translations of the Old Testament / by Harold P. Scanlin.
     p. cm.
  Includes bibliographical references and index.
  ISBN 0-8423-1010-X
  1. Dead Sea scrolls. 2. Bible. O.T.—Translating. 3. Bible.
  O.T.—Versions. 4. Paleography, Hebrew.   I. Title.
  BM487.S26 1993
  296.1'55—dc20   93-3056

Printed in the United States of America

99 98 97 96 95 94 93
8   7   6   5   4   3   2   1

Contents

DEDICATION
To Lenore

ACKNOWLEDGMENTS

A work of this nature would be impossible without the cooperation of many scholars and libraries. The Ancient Biblical Manuscript Center (Claremont, California), which maintains an archive of Dead Sea Scroll photographs, generously offered access to their collection, as well as to materials from the "Dead Sea Scroll Inventory Project," directed by Dr. Stephen A. Reed.

Others who made material available for this book are Dr. John C. Trever, who was the first to photograph the scrolls from Cave 1, and the Israel Antiquities Authority, who granted permission to reproduce a number of the scrolls. I am grateful to Nathan R. Jastram, Sidnie Ann White, and James R. Davila for granting permission to obtain copies of their dissertations. Dr. Davila also provided manuscripts of two of his forthcoming articles.

The committees responsible for the Bible translations considered here have devoted countless years to their task, often without public acclaim and little or no financial reward, but always with the sincere desire to render the Hebrew and Aramaic text of the Old Testament in an intelligible and faithful translation.

Dr. Philip W. Comfort, of Tyndale House, through his encouragement and patience, made it possible to incorporate the latest information on the scrolls. My special thanks goes to my wife, Lenore, who endured the clutter of books, papers, and photographs over many years, and can at last share in the satisfaction of seeing this project completed.

Preface

In recent years the popular press has provided many accounts of the Dead Sea Scrolls and the controversy surrounding their discovery and publication. Sensational accusations of deception and suppression, and even competing claims made by respectable scholars, have both excited and confused the public. Yet the diverse and complex nature of the evidence has sometimes made it difficult for sincere, open-minded readers to get to the heart of the issue. One of the most frequently asked questions is how do these discoveries affect the Old Testament? The writer hopes that this volume will offer a small contribution to this one aspect of Dead Sea Scroll study and to assess its impact on Bible translation.

The present work is designed to introduce the reader to the study of the text of the Old Testament found in the Dead Sea Scrolls and the impact these remarkable discoveries have had on recent Bible translations. The opening chapters bring together information on these scrolls that is scattered over a wide variety of sources. The list of biblical manuscripts is complete and their contents, with a few exceptions, are described herein. The significant variant readings among the Dead Sea Scrolls that have been taken into account by Bible translators are broadly representative, although not exhaustive.

In a work such as this there are bound to be some errors, and further examination of the manuscripts themselves may provide additional identifications or reassignments of some fragments. The author invites contributions to correct and enhance this study.

ABBREVIATIONS IN THIS WORK

General

ABMC	Ancient Biblical Manuscript Center
ASOR	American School of Oriental Research
BAS	Biblical Archaeology Society
DSS	Dead Sea Scrolls
gk/Gk	Greek Old Testament manuscripts
HOTTP	Hebrew Old Testament Text Project
IAA	Israel Antiquities Authority
LXX	Septuagint
mg	a variant reading noted in the margin of a translation
MS	manuscript
MSS	manuscripts
MT	Masoretic Text
NA²⁶	*Novum Testamentum Graece,* 26th edition
NT	New Testament
OG	Old Greek translations of the Old Testament
OT	Old Testament
p	*pesher* meaning "interpretation," a commentary on a biblical book
paleo	Hebrew manuscripts written in archaic Hebrew orthography
PAM	Palestine Archaeological Museum
pap	manuscript written on papyrus (all other manuscripts are on parchment)
TR	Textus Receptus
tg	Aramaic Targums
UBS³	*Greek New Testament,* United Bible Societies, third edition (corrected)
vid	Latin for "it appears [to read as such]"

Place Names where manuscripts were discovered

1Q	Qumran Cave 1
2Q	Qumran Cave 2
3Q	Qumran Cave 3
4Q	Qumran Cave 4
5Q	Qumran Cave 5
6Q	Qumran Cave 6
7Q	Qumran Cave 7
8Q	Qumran Cave 8
9Q	Qumran Cave 9
10Q	Qumran Cave 10
11Q	Qumran Cave 11
Hev	Nahal Hever
Mas	Masada
Mur	Murabba'at

Versions

ASV	American Standard Version
ERV	English Revised Version
GeCL	*Die Gute Nachricht*
GNB	Good News Bible
KJV	King James Version
NAB	New American Bible
NEB	New English Bible
NIV	New International Version
NJB	New Jerusalem Bible
NJV	New Jewish Version
NKJV	New King James Version
NRSV	New Revised Standard Version
REB	Revised English Bible
RSV	Revised Standard Version
TOB	*Traduction Oecuménique de la Bible*

Publications

BAR	*Biblical Archaeology Review*
BASOR	*Bulletin of the American Schools of Oriental Research*
DJD	Discoveries in the Judean Desert
ER	*A Facsimile Edition of the Dead Sea Scrolls,* Robert H. Eisenman and James M. Robinson, eds.
ALQ	*The Ancient Library of Qumran and Modern Biblical Studies,* Frank M. Cross
SWDS	*Scrolls from the Wilderness of the Dead Sea*

HEBREW TRANSLITERATIONS

Consonants

'	א
b	בּ ב
g	גּ ג
d	דּ ד
h	ה
w	ו
z	ז
ch	ח
t	ט
y	י
k	כּ כ
l	ל
m	מ
n	נ
s	ס
'	ע
p	פּ פ
ts	צ
q	ק
r	ר
s	שׂ
sh	שׁ
t	תּ ת

Vowels

a	ָ ַ
e	ֵ ֶ
e	ְ
i	ִ
o	וֹ ֹ
u	וּ ֻ

PART ONE
AN INTRODUCTION TO THE DEAD SEA SCROLLS

Secret agents using assumed names, clandestine meetings under cover of night behind enemy lines, switching cabs to avoid being followed—these sound like things in a spy novel, but they all happened in conjunction with the discovery, sale, and publication of the Dead Sea Scrolls.

The discovery of the Dead Sea Scrolls has captured the popular imagination and filled the pages of the world's newspapers with reports of alleged illegal deals, suggestions that the scrolls will shake the foundations of both Judaism and Christianity, hints of secret plots to suppress evidence—all this, combined with accusations of scholarly bickering and monopolizing texts for personal gain. It may have been inevitable that a discovery made just before the emergence of the modern state of Israel along one of its borders would have been steeped in controversy. The most recent controversy surrounding the Dead Sea Scrolls focuses primarily on the lengthy delays involving the publication of the scrolls and the related question of the motivations behind the delays. Such a situation can give rise to the suspicion that there is some plot by the people in charge to suppress documents that they find embarrassing.

This is not the first time that manuscript discoveries in the Dead Sea region have been reported. Origen (who died c. A.D. 250), as reported by the famous early church historian Eusebius (*Ecclesiastical History* 6.16), was reported to have found several different versions of Old Testament texts in the region around the Dead Sea. It is not possible to confirm Eusebius's report; but if it is true, such a discovery could have been the major factor that motivated Origen to evaluate the differences between the Hebrew text and a variety of Greek translations known in his day. Origen spent many years preparing a compilation and evaluation of the manuscripts to which he had access. His work is known as the *Hexapla* because it was arranged generally in six *(hexa)* parallel columns, which included the Hebrew text, a transliteration into Greek characters, up to five different Greek versions, and Origen's reconstruction, marked with a system of symbols to designate Greek pluses and minuses in comparison to the Hebrew text.

There was another report of a manuscript discovery in the area of the Dead Sea about the beginning of the ninth century. This discovery may be related to the origins of the Karaites, a Jewish group who relied solely on the Hebrew Bible as the authority for their belief and practice, rejecting the Oral Torah of Rabbinic Judaism, which was codified primarily in the Mishnah and Talmud. The Karaites believed that their doctrinal claim was supported by the discovery of these documents.

We will probably never know if these early reports of manuscript discoveries along the western shores of the Dead Sea are true. If the reports *are* true, the discoveries played a decisive role in the history of the Old Testament text. We do know that the Dead Sea Scrolls have brought about an equally momentous revolution in the study of the history of the Old Testament text and the religious context of the cradle of Christianity. Everyone associated with the first discovery of the scrolls immediately recognized their revolutionary importance. It is no wonder that the story of discovery and publication should be surrounded by controversy.

The details of the discovery of the Dead Sea Scrolls and the surrounding controversy have been frequently reported. Nonetheless, it is helpful to outline the important events here, focusing especially on those related to the discovery of the biblical manuscripts.

At the outset we need to keep in mind that the scrolls cannot be lumped together either geographically or by literary type. The majority of the documents popularly called the Dead Sea Scrolls were found in a single general location near the northwest shore of the Dead Sea. In all, eleven caves were found in the cliffs nearby an ancient settlement which we now know as Qumran. Of these eleven caves, ten have yielded written documents. Several of the key people mentioned in the chronological outline of events given on page 5 have published their experiences. As one might expect, there are some contradictions among the accounts, but a fascinating story emerges.

Archbishop Samuel (1966) recounts his experiences in dealing with Kando for the purchase of important scrolls from Cave 1. He also tells about efforts to resell the scrolls in his possession, ultimately leading to their purchase by Yigael Yadin in response to a brief classified ad appearing in the *Wall Street Journal* in June 1954. Yadin (1957) also recounts this transaction, as well as the earlier negotiations on behalf of Hebrew University and the Israeli government between his father, Eliezer Sukenik, and those who were offering scrolls for sale. Dr. Harry Orlinsky (1974: 245-256) tells about his involvement in the 1954 negotiations as the scholar who authenticated the antiquity and value of the scrolls purchased by Yadin. John Trever (1965a) explains the role of scholars affiliated with the American Schools of Oriental Research in Jerusalem (ASOR) in authenticating the major scrolls in the possession of Archbishop Samuel. William F. Albright, the great archaeologist and biblical scholar from Johns Hopkins University, and Millar Burrows, a general editor of the Revised Standard Version committee, were among the first to recognize the enormous significance of the scrolls. Trever, a scholar in residence at ASOR Jerusalem in the late 1940s, was an expert photographer who took the photos of the scrolls under the most trying circumstances. His photographs are still used today. The more recent controversy regarding the lack of progress in publishing the scrolls is documented in the pages of the journal *Biblical Archaeology Review*. Hershel Shanks, editor of the journal and chief advocate for prompt publication, has compiled some of the more significant articles from the *Review* (1992).

CHRONOLOGY OF EVENTS
Spring 1947 (perhaps winter 1946–1947)
Muhammed adh-Dhib discovers as many as eight scrolls in Cave 1.

April 1947?
Bedouins take scrolls to "Kando" (Khalil Iskander Shahin) in Bethlehem. Kando and his friend George Isaiah of Jerusalem probably both go to Qumran.

1947
Isaiah reports discovery of scrolls to his archbishop, Syrian Metropolitan Athanasius Y. Samuel.

June–July 1947
A meeting is arranged between Samuel and the Bedouins. Due to miscommunication, the Bedouins are not admitted to the monastery.

July 1947
Samuel buys several scrolls, including an Isaiah scroll (1QIsa[a]), the "Rule of the Community" scroll (1QS), and the Habakkuk scroll (1QpHab). The purchase probably also included 1QapGen (Apocryphon of Genesis).

Late July 1947
George Isaiah and a priest from the monastery return to Qumran and find additional fragments. Some claim other major scrolls were also discovered.

September 1947
Miles Copeland of the CIA office in Beirut photographs thirty frames of a scroll, reportedly the book of Daniel.

November 24, 1947
E. Sukenik is shown other scrolls at the Palestinian border.

November 27, 1947
Second meeting between Sukenik and those who want to sell scrolls.

November 29, 1947
Sukenik meets with sellers in Bethlehem; he is offered three scrolls. That same day the United Nations votes to form the State of Israel.

Late January 1948
Sukenik is shown Archbishop Samuel's scrolls in the YMCA, Jerusalem.

February 6, 1948
Sukenik returns scrolls to Archbishop Samuel, who then shows them to scholars at the ASOR office (now Albright Institute) in Jerusalem.

March 15, 1948
William F. Albright confirms authenticity of the scrolls.

April 11, 1948
First press release announcing the discovery of the Dead Sea Scrolls.

May 15, 1948
British mandate expires. Israeli-Arab fighting escalates.

September 1948
Sukenik publishes the first samples of scrolls he purchased for Hebrew University: Isaiah (1QIsa^b), a collection of hymns (1QH), and the "War Scroll" (1QM).

January 7, 1949
Cease-fire announced. Qumran area is in Jordanian territory.

1950
First scrolls are published by ASOR: Isaiah (1QIsa^a) and Habakkuk (1QpHab).

October 1951
More scrolls are brought to Joseph Saad of the Palestine Archaeological (now Rockefeller) Museum in Jerusalem, by Ta'amireh Bedouin. Saad launches an expedition that discovers four more caves at Wadi Murabba'at, near Qumran. R. de Vaux of the École Biblique, Jerusalem, launches an extensive archaeological expedition that continues to 1956.

6

March 20, 1952
The Copper Scroll is discovered in Cave 3.

September 1952
R. de Vaux and G. Lankester Harding discover Cave 4. Others may have removed documents earlier from this cave.

1952–1959
Fragments of the scrolls are organized in the "Scrollery" at the Rockefeller Museum in Jerusalem.

1954
Yigael Yadin (E. Sukenik's son)—former chief of staff of the Israel Defense Forces, now a professor at Hebrew University—meets with W. F. Albright while in the United States.

June 1, 1954
A short classified ad appears in the *Wall Street Journal* offering for sale "The Four Dead Sea Scrolls." Yadin sees the ad and begins to arrange for verification and possible purchase.

July 1, 1954
"Mr. Green" (a pseudonym for Dr. Harry Orlinsky) verifies the scrolls' authenticity, and Israel agrees to purchase the major scrolls belonging to Archbishop Samuel.

1955
Full publication of the Hebrew University scrolls of Isaiah ($1QIsa^b$), a collection of hymns (1QH), and the "War Scroll" (1QM) by E. Sukenik (who died in 1953).

1955
Volume 1 of Discoveries in the Judean Desert is published, containing Cave 1 manuscripts not published by ASOR or Hebrew University.

January 1956
Last Qumran cave (11) is discovered.

June 6, 1967
Israeli troops occupy the Rockefeller Museum during the Six Day War. Scrolls are still there; they were not taken to Amman, as some had thought.

1967–
Israel Department of Antiquities, now called Israel Antiquities Authority (IAA), assumes responsibility for care and publication of the Dead Sea Scrolls. The 1967 staff of scholars working on the scrolls is retained.

February 1989
In response to pressure from Hershel Shanks, editor of *Biblical Archaeology Review* (BAR), and others, IAA releases a "Suggested Timetable" for the publication of the scrolls in the Discoveries in the Judean Desert (DJD) series.

December 1990

John Strugnell, Harvard University, is replaced as chief editor of the scroll-editing team. Health reasons are cited. Others point to his recent anti-Semitic remarks as well. Emanuel Tov of Hebrew University is appointed chief editor.

September 1991

BAR publishes the text of two previously unpublished Cave 4 documents (4QD and 4QMishm), reconstructing the text from a privately held concordance compiled by scholars at "The Scrollery" in Jerusalem in the 1950s.

September 22, 1991

Huntington Library, San Marino, California, announces that their photographs of the Dead Sea Scrolls will be made available to the public.

November 20, 1991

Photographs of most of the scrolls are published by the Biblical Archaeology Society (BAS).

November 25, 1991

The Israel Antiquities Authority announces that all restrictions to the Dead Sea Scrolls have been dropped.

Early 1992

An Israeli court issues an injunction barring distribution or use of the BAS volumes of plates in "Israel and elsewhere."

October 1992

Announced date for official publication of photographs of all the scrolls in a microfiche edition by E. J. Brill publishers under the auspices of the Israel Antiquities Authority.

AVAILABILITY OF THE MANUSCRIPTS

At long last, more than forty years after the first Dead Sea Scroll discoveries, the major controversies seem to be coming to an end. All documents are now available to the scholarly world. With the appearance of the official edition of all the photographs, every library or individual can now have firsthand access to the scrolls. Many of the more controversial theories can now be put to rest. Now that we can see photograph after photograph of tiny inscribed scraps, often mixed together in a haphazard fashion, we can sympathize with the scholars who explained delays in publication on the basis of the enormity of the task, yet we will still regret that a whole generation of other scholars did not have the opportunity to study the scrolls firsthand.

The discoveries at Qumran are unquestionably the largest and most important of the finds. But in several nearby locations several miles away from Qumran along the western shore of the Dead Sea, other documents were found. These documents, while dating from the same general era, are not connected to the Qumran finds or the religious community that lived there. The other locations that have yielded biblical manuscripts will also be considered in our study of how all these manuscripts have influenced recent English translations of the Bible.

Masada is situated on top of a rock cliff overlooking the Dead Sea about fifteen miles south of En-Gedi. It is well known as the site of the final encampment of Jews who took refuge there during the Roman military conquests of A.D. 68–70. Besieged by the Roman army encamped at the base of the cliff, the residents chose suicide over surrender to the invading army. Masada had been established as a retreat fortress and was used by Herod. The rich archaeological finds included a variety of documents. Among them were several biblical manuscripts, mostly quite fragmentary, and a substantial portion of the book of Sirach.

Murabba'at is along the Dead Sea about eleven miles south of Qumran. Documents found there can be dated to the period of the Bar Kochba revolt (c. A.D. 135). Bar Kochba led an unsuccessful revolt for Jewish independence from Roman rule. Official explorations were carried out in the early months of 1952, although the caves had previously been entered in search of manuscripts. A number of biblical manuscripts were found in caves 1 and 2. The most substantial manuscript is a copy of the Minor Prophets. Fragments from Genesis, Exodus, and Numbers appear to have been from the same Torah scroll.

Caves at **Nahal Hever** (*nahal* is the Hebrew term for a river bed that fills with water during the rainy season; the Arabic term is *wadi*) were first explored in late 1953. In the spring of 1955 the Cave of Horror was discovered, so named because of the many human skeletons discovered there. Further explorations were conducted in 1960–1961. A very important Greek manuscript of the Minor Prophets was found, among other documents, in the Cave of Horror. The Cave of the Letters, discovered in the 1960–1961 season, yielded a few biblical scrolls, although there is no clear evidence that they were stored in this cave in antiquity. They may have been left there in modern times by Bedouins while exploring the caves in the area in search of manuscripts that could be sold.

Over eight hundred manuscripts have been discovered in the caves at

Qumran. The vast majority of the manuscripts are poorly preserved. Often only a few columns of text survive, many times only a few barely legible scraps can be identified; but the quantity of material offers a treasure of information from a period and region that previously yielded little manuscript evidence. There are about 250 Qumran biblical manuscripts, mostly in Hebrew, but some in Aramaic and Greek. The rest of the manuscripts are copies of nonbiblical documents, many of which we previously knew nothing about. Many of these compositions are closely related to the biblical text but are not strictly Bible manuscripts. These include biblical commentaries called *pesharim,* which contain excerpts of the biblical text followed by the Hebrew word *pesher,* "its meaning." There were also biblical paraphrases and collections of biblical quotations related to a specific topic. A number of phylacteries were also found among the Dead Sea Scrolls. Phylacteries are selected biblical passages from Deuteronomy and Exodus, written in a very small handwriting and worn by the devout in the form of tied capsules as a reminder of the importance of the Law.

There is a difference of opinion among scholars as to whether the biblical manuscripts or the newly discovered nonbiblical texts (which deal with the religious teachings and biblical interpretation of the Qumran community) are more important. Baigent and Leigh (1991:40), citing R. H. Eisenman, maintain that the biblical material is "perfectly innocuous and uncontroversial, containing no revelations of any kind. It consists of little more than copies of books from the Old Testament, more or less the same as those already in print or with only minor alterations." On the other hand, James Sanders (1992:329), a leading biblical scholar, maintains that "the area of study which has perhaps been most affected by the scrolls is first [Old] Testament text criticism." These radically different points of view can be explained in part by the fact that Baigent and Leigh believe that there is some conspiracy to suppress Qumran documents that would presumably be embarrassing to those who are blocking publication. On the other hand, Sanders' academic specialty is textual criticism; so naturally we would expect that he would find a great deal of interest in the biblical manuscripts among the Dead Sea Scrolls.

The conspiracy theory has gained little support in the academic community. Even Hershel Shanks (1992:275-290), editor of *Biblical Archaeology Review* and chief champion of the recent drive to publish the Dead Sea

Scrolls, discounts the conspiracy theory as a reason for the lengthy delay in publishing the scrolls.

On the other hand, the importance of the biblical manuscripts for the recovery of the best text of the Old Testament has been recognized from the outset. The first scroll to be published was the nearly complete scroll of the book of Isaiah (1QIsa[a]). Scholars were immediately struck by the fact that in many ways it corresponded to the great medieval manuscripts of the Old Testament, all of which are at least a thousand years later than the Dead Sea Scrolls. But they were also intrigued by a number of different readings in the manuscript and the spelling system used by the scribes. The earliest forms of Hebrew writing use few, if any, vowels. However, to aid the reader and ensure that potentially ambiguous words and phrases be correctly read and understood, scribes gradually added more and more vowels. This was done less frequently in Bible manuscripts than in non-biblical material, but 1QIsa[a] incorporated the fuller spelling system, suggesting that this manuscript was designed for easier reading by resolving the potential ambiguities created by the lack of vowels in the text.

Rumors still persist that other manuscripts from the Dead Sea were discovered since 1947 and are being held secretly. According to the rumors, either the holders of the documents are waiting for an opportune time to sell their treasures at the highest possible profit, or they fear that making the documents public will bring legal action against them from the antiquities authorities. It is also claimed by some that certain documents are being suppressed by religious authorities because they fear that the contents would be damaging to their beliefs. The conspiracy theory has most recently been argued by Baigent and Leigh in *The Dead Sea Scrolls Deception* (1991), but Hershel Shanks of the *Biblical Archaeology Review,* perhaps the most outspoken critic of the official handling of the scrolls, doubts that there is any conspiracy afoot. The Vatican and some of the Roman Catholic scholars on the official team are the objects of the sharpest criticism from Baigent and Leigh, whose conspiracy claims cannot be substantiated and are contradicted by the general openness of the Roman Catholic, Protestant, and Jewish scholars who have studied the sectarian documents. While the existence of the rumored other documents cannot be ruled out, it must be said that there is no firm evidence for their existence.

The controversy concerning failure to publish the scrolls in a timely fashion has focused almost exclusively on the nonbiblical manuscripts.

However, some reports in the popular press have given the general public the impression that the unpublished material *includes* biblical manuscripts, saying that some of them may contain evidence of readings that are significantly different from known biblical manuscripts. While some biblical manuscripts have not as yet been published, the vast majority of them have. In the case of some of the very fragmentary biblical scrolls from Cave 4, the manuscript evidence has been available to the general academic community through a series of doctoral dissertations, especially those given at Harvard University under Frank M. Cross. Some critics of the scrolls' publication committee have complained about the committee members' practice of making manuscript material available for doctoral research through only their own academic institutions. Regardless of one's opinion on this issue, the biblical scrolls have been made available.

The piecing together of biblical fragments is helped in part by the fact that, since the scholars were dealing with documents whose general contents are already known, they are less difficult to reconstruct. Concordances, both printed and electronic, are a great help in determining where particular fragments may fit. It is very time-consuming to piece together nonbiblical fragments and then make sense of them.

DATING THE MANUSCRIPTS

The dating of biblical manuscripts is crucial for their proper evaluation and consequent determination of their worth for textual criticism. One factor for determining the age of manuscripts is the archaeological environment in which they were found. For example, around A.D. 70 Qumran was destroyed during the Jewish war and Roman invasion. Thus, assuming that the Dead Sea Scrolls found near the Qumran settlement were the product of that community, then the latest date for the manuscripts hidden in nearby caves is A.D. 70. Although some scholars still question the connection of the Qumran community with the caves (for example: Golb, 1980), most agree that the connection is firmly established and that the manuscripts can safely be assumed to have been written no later than the middle of the first century A.D.

Analysis of the minute details of the style of writing, known as paleography, cannot only corroborate the archaeological evidence for the latest date of the manuscripts, it can also help to estimate the age of the individual manuscripts. It must be recognized that paleography is not an exact science, but an art, even though modern technological advances have greatly enhanced the reliability and precision of paleographic studies. Recent innovations such as digitally enhanced computer-graphic images have enabled paleographers to be more certain about some readings in manuscripts that have fallen victim to deterioration and wear. When the Dead Sea Scrolls were first discovered, special infrared photography was also available to enhance the legibility of faded or browned manuscripts. Computer concordances have also aided greatly in identifying possible locations of biblical fragments of scrolls. For example, if only a few letters from each of two lines appear under each other in a tiny fragment, a computer concordance can give the researcher a list of possible biblical passages where these letter sequences occur within the limits of two lines of text.

Paleography's major contribution is the establishment of a sequence of script development based on the fundamental principle that handwriting tends to evolve over the years by changing the styles and shapes of individual letters. Just as language itself changes over the years, due both to external and internal influences, handwriting also changes. One only needs to compare contemporary handwriting with the Victorian style of the nineteenth century or the styles of earlier centuries to realize that English styles of handwriting have changed. When the analysis of changing styles establishes relative sequences, that knowledge is combined with other documents that can be dated by other means (such as historically datable references within the documents or established datable archaeological contexts), and the paleographer can establish both a firm range of dates and a relative sequence within these dates. Paleographers who have worked on the Dead Sea Scrolls have utilized datable inscriptions such as coins from the Hasmonean era, the era in Palestinian Jewish history that began with the military victory of the Maccabees. These coins, with their inscriptions, are described in a number of catalogs of ancient Jewish coins, including Meshorer (1967) and Kindler (1974).

Another important manuscript used for comparative paleographic studies is the Nash papyrus, which contains the Ten Commandments derived from both the Exodus and Deuteronomy texts. Prior to the discovery of the Dead Sea Scrolls, it was the earliest known copy of any portion of the Old Testament. The early form of the handwriting, dated to the second century B.C. by William F. Albright (1949), was one of the basic tools that was first used to date the Dead Sea Scrolls.

A pioneering paleographical study of the earliest recovered Dead Sea Scrolls was done by Solomon A. Birnbaum, *The Qumran (Dead Sea) Scrolls and Palaeography* (1952), dealing with the manuscripts from Cave 1 and comparing them with other writing from the general period.

Birnbaum, a recognized paleographer, effectively argued against Solomon Zeitlin and others, who considered the Dead Sea Scrolls the product of the Middle Ages. Malachi Martin, in a massive two-volume study entitled *The Scribal Character of the Dead Sea Scrolls* (1958), offered a detailed study of the scribal habits of the scribes of the Dead Sea Scrolls. He dealt with the major manuscript finds from Cave 1: 1QIsa^a, 1QIsa^b, 1QpHab, and the nonbiblical manuscripts 1QH, 1QM, and 1QS. The most important study of the Dead Sea Scroll scripts, considering manuscript evidence from many of the caves, is Frank M. Cross's "The Development of the Jewish Scripts" (1961). His work remains the standard point of reference for paleographic dating of the Qumran manuscripts.

In this book we will follow Cross's general outline of the development of the Hebrew scripts of the Dead Sea Scrolls, recognizing that exact dating is not possible, but that most dates can be considered accurate within twenty-five or fifty years, and that Qumran manuscripts are no later than A.D. 70. (It is possible that a few manuscripts may have found their way into the Qumran collection, either by placement in the caves in antiquity or by recent intermixing. One possible example is 4QGen^b, which may have been brought to Cave 4 by the Bedouin from Murabba'at, according to Davila [1990:5].)

Specific details on how paleography has effected the dating of the Dead Sea Scrolls are given in part two (p. 41), and further discussion on the dating of the Dead Sea Scrolls can be found in the following publications:

Stegemann, Hartmut. "Methods for the Reconstruction of Scrolls from Scattered Fragments" in *Archaeology and History in the Dead Sea Scrolls,* L. H. Schiffman, editor, pp. 189-220.

Wahl, Thomas. "How Did the Hebrew Scribe Form His Letters?" *Journal of the Ancient Near Eastern Society of Columbia University* 3 (1971:8-20).

Yardeni, Ada. "The Palaeography of 4QJer^b—a Comparative Study" in *Textus* 15 (1990:233-268).

Any lingering doubts about the age of the Dead Sea Scrolls can now be dismissed because of the results of recent radiocarbon tests using the accelerator mass-spectrometry technique. Early Carbon 14 tests were done on associated material, rather than the scrolls themselves, because the amount of material that had been needed to run the tests would have destroyed too much of the manuscripts. Newer techniques now require far less material, so it was possible to test samples taken directly from fourteen manuscripts from four sites in the Dead Sea area. All but one of the manuscripts tested are within the range of dates given by paleographers. The one anomaly was a nonbiblical Qumran manuscript whose Carbon 14 date was two hundred years older than paleographic dating. In this case there appears to be evidence of some physical contamination. The biblical manuscripts tested were 1QIsa^a and 4QSam^c (Bonani:1991).

THE DEAD SEA SCROLLS AND MODERN TRANSLATIONS OF THE OLD TESTAMENT

Bible translators are faced not only with the issue of obtaining manu-script evidence from the Dead Sea Scrolls (and elsewhere) but also with how this evidence can actually be used in making new translations and/or revising old ones. The traditional assumption of most translators was that in general the best available avenue back to the "original text" of the Old Testament was through the Masoretic Text (MT). Neverthe-less, translators have generally accepted the view that to a greater or lesser degree there are still problems in the Masoretic Text as preserved in the great medieval codices such as *Codex Leningradensis,* used as the basis of *Biblia Hebraica Stuttgartensia* and the Aleppo Codex, the basis of the "Hebrew University Bible Project." In some cases difficult Hebrew constructions that puzzle modern translators were problematic for ancient translators as well. In such situations Ellington (1989:22-25) proposed a "consensus system" for making textual decisions by follow-ing the majority vote of five major modern translations: Revised Stand-ard Version (RSV), New American Bible (NAB), Today's English Version (TEV), New International Version (NIV), and the New Jewish Version (NJV). Osborn (1981) proposed a similar consensus approach. But this method, despite Ellington's belief that it is an objective system, fails to take into account the fact that our understanding of the textual history of the Old Testament is being completely revised in light of the Dead Sea Scroll discoveries.

Each of the five major translations selected for consideration differs in its understanding of Old Testament textual history. The RSV can be said to reflect the consensus view of mid-century textual scholars. The NAB accepts the three-recension theory of Frank M. Cross, at times showing a definite preference for the Egyptian recension as witnessed by the agreement of LXX and some Qumran manuscripts. This is especially evident in its translation of the books of Samuel. The TEV may be said to take a mediating position somewhere between the RSV and the NAB, although the translators' access to the Qumran evidence was significantly less extensive than the NAB's. The NJV offers a translation of the "traditional text" of Judaism, i.e., the Masoretic Text, with its antecedents in the most stable of the earliest witnesses, notably the proto-MT. The NIV also holds the MT in high regard, but is willing to depart from it not only in cases where the translators concluded that the MT was corrupt, but also in cases where a less-well-attested witness yields a translation more in harmony with a New Testament quotation or allusion (e.g., Ps. 2:9/Rev. 2:27; Ps. 116:10/2 Cor. 4.13). Bruce Waltke, one of the NIV translators, explained this "harmonization principle" (Barker 1986:89), but in a more recent article expressed reservations about this practice (1989:26).

Some reviewers have complained that, despite the extensive selection of textual problems dealing primarily with translation issues, a number of important items have not been considered by the Hebrew Old Testament Text Project (HOTTP) (Klein 1985). But just as the UBS[3] Greek New Testament does not promise to present a whole range of textual problems in its critical apparatus, instead choosing primarily those of interest to translators, HOTTP is intended to aid translators in their task. Yet Klein points out that the HOTTP discusses only seven readings for 1 Samuel 10, preferring the MT in all but one case. In this same chapter the NRSV departs from the MT six times. In 1 Samuel 1:1–2:10 the contrast between the HOTTP's textual decisions and the NRSV textual base is even more evident. The HOTTP considers eight passages, diverging from MT in two of them, while NRSV departs from MT in eight additional passages. Of course, the HOTTP committee could not have been expected to anticipate the textual decisions made by the NRSV committee, but the increase in the number of MT departures suggests that text-critical considerations have increased in recent years.

OLD TESTAMENT TEXTUAL THEORIES

To understand the significance of the changes in approaching textual issues in recent translations it is important to recognize the profound changes that have occurred in our understanding of the textual history of the Old Testament. These profound and fundamental changes are at least as significant as the revolution in New Testament textual criticism in the late nineteenth century, which culminated in the work of Westcott and Hort.

In the latter half of the nineteenth century Paul de Lagarde advocated a one-recension theory to account for textual variation in the Old Testament, based primarily on the high degree of consistency in the Hebrew text of the many manuscripts collated by Kennicott and de Rossi. Lagarde's one-recension archetype manuscript reached back to the first century of the common era. Lagarde also proposed a similar situation for the Septuagint. From a single translation three recensions developed, namely those of Origen, Lucian, and Hesychius, each with implicit geographic orientation. Lagarde did not work out his theories for the entire corpus of the Hebrew Bible and the Septuagint. He did, however, publish a critically recon-structed text of what he believed to be the Lucianic recension of Genesis to Esther in his *Librorum Veteris Testamenti Canonicorum pars prior* (Goöttingen, 1883).

Paul Kahle (1959), taking his cue from the ancient Letter of Aristeas, which narrates the story of the great Greek translation of the Pentateuch undertaken in Alexandria, maintained that there were many old Greek translations of the nature of *Targumim* that the translation of "the Seventy" (i.e., *Septuaginta*) was intended to supplant. But the plurality of text types persisted until the emergence of the three major recensions that had devel-oped by the time of Origen, and which related to his work on the Hexapla.

Of course, the work of Lagarde antedated the Dead Sea Scroll discover-ies, and Kahle developed his theories long before that time, although in his later years he attempted to show that the textual evidence of the Dead Sea Scrolls could be made to conform to his theory. By the 1950s the major issues were raised and the groundwork laid for thinking within a frame-work of recensions, text types, and geographic distribution. Frank M. Cross (1975a, 1975b), the first official editor assigned most of the Cave 4 biblical manuscripts, formulated a three-recension or text-type theory with geographic orientation in Egypt (LXX), Palestine (Samaritan Pentateuch), and Babylon (proto-Masoretic Text). These labels are only an approximation of the textual witnesses, but Cross's theory was quite influential in shaping the discussion about textual witnesses.

Dominique Barthélemy entered into the discussion with his work on the important Greek Minor Prophets scroll found at Nahal Hever. This manuscript, dating from the turn of the era, is a pre-Christian recension of the Old Greek (OG) translation. Its revisions are characteristic of the *kaige* recension and are described as proto-Theodotionic, bringing the text into line with the proto-Masoretic Text in a number of ways. This Palestinian tradition differs from the recensional activity of the early Greek church fathers.

Shemaryahu Talmon (1975, 1989) modified Cross's text-type theory by pointing to sociological groups—rather than geographic areas—as the locus of text types or text groups. These *Gruppentexte* developed within the diversity of Judaism at the time. Three major recensions, or text groups, survived because the groups that preserved them survived—namely orthodox Judaism (proto-Masoretic Text), Samaritans (Samaritan Pentateuch), and Christians, who appropriated the Septuagint as their edition of the Old Testament.

Emanuel Tov (1980:64-65) has commented on the mixed nature of some important Qumran biblical manuscripts:

> We suggest that the Samuel scrolls from Cave 4, 11QpaleoLev, as well as many other texts from Qumran, reflect such early texts [not three recensions] of the OT, insofar as they do not agree exclusively with one tradition, but agree now with this and then with that text (MT, LXX, and Samaritan Pentateuch), and in addition contain a significant number of exclusive readings. In our view, the traditional characterization of the LXX as a text type is imprecise and misleading. In the case of the Samuel scrolls, the recognition of a relatively large number of "LXX readings" made it easy for scholars to label some of these scrolls as "Septuagintal," and this characterization was readily accepted in scholarship which had become used to viewing the textual witnesses of the OT as belonging to three main streams. However, . . . this view should now be considered outdated.

For several books there is clear evidence of at least two ancient editions (Scanlin 1988:211-213), but the great degree of admixture of what appears to be two editions of Samuel has prompted Ulrich (1988:103-105) to recommend that a translation of Samuel should select now one and now another text from the double literary tradition:

> For 1 Samuel 1–2 we find in the earlier edition (the MT I would pre-liminarily suggest) a straightforward account with one portrait of Hannah. In the secondary edition (the LXX) we find the intentional and consistent reshaping of that account, arguably for theological motives and possibly for misogynous motives, to give a changed portrait of Hannah. When we turn to 1 Samuel 17–18, in the earlier edition (the LXX) we find a single version of the story, whereas in the secondary edition (the MT) we find a composite version.

Which edition should be translated? Ulrich (1988:112-113) believes that "a decision to translate the form preserved in the MT can be made legiti-mately in principle (*a priori*). . . . A decision in principle to translate the MT specifically is completely legitimate and desirable, on both scholarly and religious grounds." This is the decision of the NJV. Ulrich correctly goes on to say that an analogous argument for a translation of the LXX can also be made. This, in fact, is being done by Marguerite Harl and others in *La Bible d'Alexandrie* (Paris:Cerf, 1986–). To date, Genesis, Exodus, Leviticus, and Deuteronomy have been published. But, Ulrich concludes:

> If we were to decide that the textual basis of our translation should be the earliest careful edition of a text . . . preserved in our witnesses, then we should choose different editions for different books and units within certain books. For 1 Samuel we would choose MT for the Hannah story and the Old Greek tradition (OG) for the David and Goliath story. If, on the other hand, we were to decide that the textual basis of our translation should be the latest careful edition of a text accepted as authoritative by a community, then we should select the MT for David and Goliath and the OG for the Hannah story.

James Sanders discusses these issues within the framework of "canon criticism," in which he sees as crucial the period of intense stabilization of the authoritative literature by a believing community. According to Sand-ers (1991:205-206):

> The task of text criticism is the quest for the most critically responsi-ble text. But such a formulation is not in itself clear enough: for obviously this cannot mean simply accepting, or even putting excep-tional value on, the earliest texts we have; they exhibit a consider-

able fluidity. Nor should it mean that text criticism throws in the towel and accepts willy-nilly a *textus receptus.*

The practical implications of such an approach may mean, for example, if one accepts the LXX reading, which has Qumran support, at Isaiah 40:6a, ("and I replied" for "and one replied"), a structural-literary analysis of the entire passage supports the acceptance of the LXX variant in Isaiah 40:2, which lacks any Hebrew support. Instead of mixing the literary traditions, Sanders suggests that it may be possible to offer a translation of both texts of Isaiah 40:1-11 in parallel columns (1991:212-213), although the presentation of pluriform texts in a Bible translation intended for the general public is certainly problematic.

The critical point at hand is this: Is the recent trend toward a new respect for the Masoretic Text a retreat to the centuries-old preference for the Masoretic Text of the Rabbinic Bibles? This is the criticism offered by some, such as B. Albrektson (1975), who have examined the principles underlying the work of the Hebrew Old Testament Text Project, which is sponsored by the United Bible Societies for the purpose of assisting their Bible translators. Two related major criticisms have been expressed: (1) the HOTTP committee's preponderant preference for the Masoretic Text (MT), and (2) their failure to give due consideration to conjectural emendations (i.e., corrections made to the text on the basis of scholarly conjecture without having any actual manuscript support). But, did the committee actually "exclude conjectures from consideration" (Barr 1988:447; Albrektson 1981:1-18)? The reviewers surely did not mean that Barthélemy's treatment neglected the discussion of conjectural emendations. Even a casual reading of the first three of five published volumes of the final reports of the committee, *Critique textuelle de l'Ancien Testament,* will show that proposed emendations are discussed at length. Barr's statement suggests otherwise. I suspect that Barr is criticizing the failure of the HOTTP to give due consideration to emendation as a means of restoring the text. But others have expressed greater appreciation for HOTTP's general preference for the harder reading. For example, Robert Hanhart (1985:145-146) said:

> With regard to internal evidence, the Committee rightly shows great appreciation for the old principle of *lectio difficilior* (i.e., a difficult variant reading is more likely original than an easier reading). It also

has a higher regard for the syntactical methods of analysis and interpretation used by the most ancient Jewish and Christian exegetes
than it does for the methods of modern exegesis. . . . A conjecture
must not be put forward out of laziness, but there are times when it
is logical to make a particular conjecture on the basis of evidence
gleaned from a careful comparison of the traditional text forms.

TEXTUAL CRITICISM AND TRANSLATION PRAXIS

But the crucial question remains: What text do we translate? Is the primary focus of interest the *Urtext* (the original text in its earliest written
form) or a later canonical form of the text? To understand this question,
readers should know that the HOTTP describes the development of the
Old Testament text in four stages. The first stage is the Urtext for which
there is no documentary evidence. The second stage begins with the
intense stabilization process that spans the last centuries B.C. down through
A.D. 70. This stabilization process was carried out in different ways by different religious communities and even varied in certain books of the Old
Testament. The third period is marked by the emergence of a received text
which, because of its dominance, largely if not completely eliminated
other readings and forms of the text within the religious communities that
agreed on a received text. The stabilization process seems to have dealt
with a minimum residue of textual variants by allowing both readings to
be preserved in the received text. There appears to be at least one function
of the *kethib-qere* marginal system (i.e., the reading of the text with an
alternate reading in the margin) still preserved in the Masoretic Text. The
final stage is the emergence of the Masoretic Text by about A.D. 1000.
Other text critics have described the development of the Old Testament
text in a different series of stages. (See the chart on pp. 36-37.) Despite the
differences, there is agreement on the crucial importance of stage-two
developments.

B. Albrektson (1978:50), one of the first outspoken critics of the
HOTTP's policy regarding emendation, ascribes little normative value to a
stage-two or -three text, since he questions whether "the emergence of the
standard text must have been the result of a conscious and deliberate text-
critical activity with the purpose of creating a normative recension."
Albrektson's primary concern is the denial of any text-critical activity by
the Jewish authorities during this critical period; this denial also implies

21

that no text of the period was given the impetus towards normativeness by the religious community.

On the other hand, James Sanders (1987:163) says "criticism has felt free to rewrite the text in the light of what it could bring to study of the text in an effort to reconstruct an Urtext," and in so doing has "shifted the locus of authority from what the early believing communities received, shaped, and passed on, to what scholars were convinced was said or written in the first place. What perhaps had started as a historian's exercise . . . became a focus of authority." Barr (1988:140) strenuously objects to Sanders's sloganeering phrase "rewriting the Bible," but he seems to fall victim to the same temptation when he says that Sanders (and, by implication, the HOTTP committee) would not even "allow [textual emendation] to be mentioned."

Surprisingly, Old Testament critics, whose names are virtually synonymous with emendation and reconstruction of the Urtext, were themselves cautious when dealing with the question of the textual basis of Old Testament translation. G. F. Moore (1900:23), in the notes to his critical edition of Judges in the Polychrome Bible, says, "The task of the textual critic is not to restore the text of the *sources* [emphasis his], nor even of some earlier state of the composite work, but only the form in which it left the hand of the last redactor."

The American committee responsible for producing an American edition of the English Revised Version (ERV, 1885), resulting in the publication of the American Standard Version (ASV, 1901), were sensitive to the criticism that the ERV adhered too closely to the Masoretic Text. In light of this criticism they decided to solicit the opinions of a number of eminent German Old Testament scholars, including Dillmann, Kautzsch, Strack, and Wellhausen. Wellhausen (1886:55-56) responded:

> That a reading of the LXX is in itself worth exactly as much as the corresponding one in the Massoretic text, is obvious. The grounds for preferring the one or the other are, however, always only internal—equally so whether that of the LXX or that of the Massoretic text is preferred. Furthermore, it is my opinion that, as the sanctity of the Bible is derived from its recognition by the church, the church must also determine for itself *which* Bible, i.e., to which text of the Bible, it will accord this sanctity.

Wellhausen had presented his opinion more fully in his revision of the fourth edition of Bleek's introduction to the Old Testament, section 284. Wellhausen (1871:14, note) believed that conjectural emendation does not serve well to recover some intermediate stage in the evolution from arche-type to recensions, but aims at reconstructing the original text form, since only truth can testify on its own behalf. On the other hand, H. P. Smith (1885:623), in criticizing the textual base of the English Revised Version, was convinced that "an existing copy of an ancient book is of value to us only so far as it represents its original." Since he goes on immediately to talk about the autographs (the original writings), it must be assumed that this is what he means by original, not merely the *Vorlage* (the prototype manuscript from which others are made) of a particular text family.

Barthélemy (1982:*76) addressed the issue of textual criticism as it per-tains to recovering the original wording or reconstrucing the text in its sec-ond stage. He summarized the framework within which the HOTTP operates:

> It is that original framework which provides the internal evidence for conjectural emendation and which can therefore be its only aim. As long as textual criticism aims at recovering the original literary framework of a text, it will be both necessary and appropriate to appeal to conjectural emendation. If, however, the aim is to arrive at the text as it stood at the beginning of the second period of its devel-opment, conjectural emendation runs the risk of overshooting this aim and recovering a textual form appropriate to the first phase.

But what of Barr's (and others') objection that in cases where the MT seems hopelessly corrupt it seems absurd to struggle to make sense of what is clearly in error rather than to resort to a plausible emendation? Barr asks whether this approach leads to a belief that "error, so long as we have it on paper, is better than truth that is not on paper" (1988:140). But Barr's dichotomy between "error" and "truth" casts too wide a net—or at least it will be understood by many to do so. In cases where "hopelessly corrupt" means that we moderns are at a total loss to make sense out of the existing MT, we must hazard a guess at its meaning and frankly acknowl-edge our puzzlement in a footnote. Even the NJV reverts to this type of solution on occasion.

Yet at what point do we declare the MT to be hopelessly corrupt? Ander-sen and Freedman, in the Anchor Bible, translated the entire book of Hosea (recognized as being full of thorny problems) by following the MT in virtually every case! And if by hopelessly corrupt we mean that in the course of the editorial and redactional development of particular books the thread of the discourse was altered (garbled?), then Barthélemy's objection (1982:*76) to emendation is particularly valid: "Is one to use conjectural emendation to eliminate an ancient text because it has been restructured to provide a new context that gives meaning to a redactor's insertion?" He goes on to say, "In dealing with composite texts such as we find in the Pentateuch or Chronicles, a textual criticism based on conjectural emendation threatens to shatter the fragile unity which the redactor tried to piece together out of diverse materials."

Dealing with the stage-two text is not a matter of despair over the chimera of reconstructing the Urtext, it is rather a positive recognition that we are dealing with the "church's book." It is not only their original literary forms that give these texts authority, but a corpus that admittedly took new shapes and forms—at times minor and at other times more extensive. Thus, a form of the text that is "wrong" (= secondary) on literary grounds may be authoritative as canon, and to be preferred to a conjectural text that may "have every possibility of being literarily correct but for which there is no evidence that it functioned as sacred scripture for any community" (Barthélemy 1982:*77).

It is, therefore, necessary to distinguish between those early readings that can be recognized as deriving from the perils of textual transmission and those that are the result of ancient editorial or recensional activity. Emanuel Tov (1981:307-308) goes so far as to say:

> No early reading should be 'preferred' to another, because variants like those analyzed [in the previous chapter of his book] derive from a certain stage in the literary growth of the biblical books and as such they cannot and should not be preferred to readings belonging to another stage in the literary development of these books.

In Tov's view "there exist *no relevant external considerations* [author's emphasis] that can be applied to the evaluation of readings retroverted from the ancient versions" (1981:286), although he would allow for a few exceptions from some Hebrew sources. Although Tov's position may seem extreme, it does serve to emphasize the importance of recognizing the nature of the literary and textual evolution of the Old Testament.

Barthélemy, in an important article in *De Septuaginta: Studies in Hon-*

24

our of John William Wevers (1984:19-41), discusses the whole matter of the relationship of literary and textual criticism and concludes with an outline of the proper use by the exegete (and translator) of the LXX:

TEXTUAL CRITICISM OF THE MT AND THE LXX

a) When the text of a passage that is difficult or textually defective gives rise to a new text intended to correct the old, this literary phenomenon deserves to be studied carefully, but the text in question should not be changed.

b) The MT is a text which has been only slightly altered in the ways described above. This renders it readily amenable to further alteration. Chances are that the defective passages remain intact in the text, and one rarely has to worry about destroying a new literary structure in the process of restoring the text.

c) The LXX (along with the Samaritan) began to diverge from the predecessors of the MT at a much earlier date than any other text. Because of this, the LXX is best able to testify as to the earlier state of the MT, before the accumulation of accidental changes had altered the text.

d) It is necessary to keep in mind that the LXX (and often its Vorlage) is textually much more innovative than the MT. When the LXX seems to have preserved a coherent text (in cases where the MT is almost certainly defective), then it is necessary to recognize the possibility that this apparent coherence of the LXX was obtained by way of correction (occasionally even in its Vorlage), starting from a defective form which the MT has preserved without alteration.

e) When we say that the textual critic would be right in correcting accidental errors which have not undergone the sort of literary correction described above, it is important to keep in mind that an extreme case is being described.

Recent translations of 1 Samuel have diverged widely in their willingness to depart from the MT. This is not only a matter of the degree of confidence the translation committees held towards the MT, but also reflects the complex state of the text of 1 Samuel in its variety of forms during the period of the emergence of the stage-two text. Put one way, it may be claimed that the text of 1 Samuel has suffered greatly in transmission; or one may conclude that two editions of 1 Samuel existed in antiquity and that the degree of admixture between these editions may be seen in the extant forms of the text. A translation such as the NIV, with only fifteen MT departures in 1 Samuel, demonstrates its reverence for the MT. At the other end of the scale, the NAB departs about 230 times, many departures being based on the Qumran evidence and its frequent support of LXX readings. The departures from the MT in 1 Samuel in the following translations provide a full picture:

New International Version: 15
Today's English Version: 51
Revised Standard Version: about 60
New Revised Standard Version: about 110
New English Bible: 160
New American Bible: 230

Statistics on earlier translations are taken from Albrektson (1981:17).

In the account of the early achievements of Saul in 1 Samuel 9:27–11:1 (anointing, proclamation as king, military accomplishments), there are a number of significant pluses in the OG that add certain details which generally reinforce a positive view of Saul's kingship. In 10:1, Samuel prophesies that Saul will save Israel from their enemies. And 10:21 describes the selection process in greater detail than the MT by saying that the men of the Matrite family were brought forth one by one, reinforcing the point that a man-by-man search for the chosen king was carried out to no avail, since Saul was hiding. The final major plus (10:27) offers a full explanation of the gravity of the threat by Nahash, king of the Ammonites. Any Israelite who crossed the Jordan into Ammonite territory had his right eye gouged out, and Israel had "no deliverer." Thus Saul's courage and military prowess would be recognized as a particularly notable achievement and a specific fulfillment of Samuel's promise in 10:1 (OG) that Saul will save Israel from the hand of their enemies. The addition to 10:27 is not attested in the OG, but is found in 4QSam[a], as well as in Josephus's *Antiquities* (6.5.1), where Josephus offers the further explanation that gouging out only the right eye was sufficient to disable a warrior, since his shield would cover the left eye anyway.

If the addition to 10:1 is considered a gloss, then the balance of the related textual problems would favor MT, which is precisely the decision made by the Hebrew Old Testament Text Project. However, if one accepts the OG reading of 10:1 (as in RSV, NRSV, NAB, and NEB), then the fuller 10:21 and the different form of the question in 10:22, which is more appropriate in light of the fuller 10:21, follow. Since the fuller 10:27 was poorly attested in external evidence (primarily Josephus) prior to the Qumran discovery, it is not surprising that RSV did not add it. However,

NAB ventures a footnote, "There is ancient evidence for a longer introduction to this campaign," and cite 4QSam[a] in their "Textual Notes," published in some editions. NRSV now places the extra material in the text, completing the process of accepting the OG version of the narrative, with an attested Hebrew *Vorlage* for at least one of the additions. One should keep in mind that the Qumran evidence in this section is fragmentary. Nothing is known about its witness to the text of the earlier section of the narrative. This may be construed as an admittedly weak *ex silentio* argument in favor of the OG/Qumran version. But it must be remembered that a comparison of all extant sections of 4QSam[a] shows that it is not consistent in its preference for the OG (Tov: 1980).

Rofé (1982:131), in rejecting the originality of the fuller text, points out that it is a typical Midrashic duplication that may add clarity in one respect, but loses even more in another. K. Luke (1986:211), on the other hand, argues for its inclusion primarily on the ground that "to the historian, v 27b is of the highest interest."

It would seem that there are only two options for the translator. One could follow the version attested in the MT as done in NJV and NIV (as well as TOB and GeCL), or the entire set of OG variants could be followed (with partial support from 4QSam[a]), including 10:22, "Did the man come here?"—an appropriate question following the man-by-man review which was expected to reveal the chosen king. The HOTTP recommends 4QSam[a] *t[e]nupot* (wave offerings) for 10:4, which is the reading in the OG and which is also used by NAB.

In summary, the underlying theoretical basis for the history of the OT text and the praxis of textual criticism needs to be recognized. Although textual scholars may differ in the assumptions they make about the history of the text, valid comparisons can only be made if these presuppositions are made clear.

THE EFFECT OF THE DEAD SEA SCROLLS ON MODERN TRANSLATIONS OF THE OLD TESTAMENT

Every major Bible translation published since 1950 has claimed to have taken into account the textual evidence of the Dead Sea Scrolls. Naturally, they could only utilize the evidence made available by the time of their work. After the initial publication of 1QIsa[a], 1QIsa[b], and 1QpHab utilized by the RSV, additional manuscript evidence was rather meager and slow to be utilized by other translation teams. This was due in part to the relative inaccessibility of the material as well as its limited quantity. Gradually, however, translations undertaken in the 1960s and 1970s considered whatever evidence was available to them. The evidence was utilized not only to marshall evidence for or against a particular textual reading but to come to a better understanding of the history of the transmission of the Old Testament text.

The official statements of the translators regarding their attitude toward text-critical issues can provide insight into the translators' attitude toward the Masoretic Text and the other ancient witnesses. We can also see a shifting attitude, especially in cases where major revisions of recent translations have appeared, e.g.: the Revised Standard Version (1952) and the New Revised Standard Version (1990); the New English Bible (1970); and the Revised English Bible (1989). The New American Bible, first published in 1970, is currently undergoing a major revision. The revised New Testament appeared in 1986; to date only the revised Psalms has been published (1992). The Jerusalem Bible (1966) has been superseded by the New Jerusalem Bible (1985). Each committee had a variety of reasons for undertaking a revision in a relatively short period of time, especially when compared to the general history of Bible translation. But all the revisions have taken the opportunity to reassess the value of the Dead Sea Scrolls in their work.

The work of the RSV translation committee was well underway when the first of the Qumran manuscript discoveries came to the attention of the scholarly world in 1948. Millar Burrows, a member of the RSV Old Testament committee, edited and published (1950) the first group of manuscripts that at the time were in the possession of Archbishop Athanasius Y. Samuel, including both 1QIsa^a and 1QpHab. Burrows also wrote two books that were largely responsible for introducing the Dead Sea Scrolls to the general public. In *The Dead Sea Scrolls* (1955) and its sequel, *More Light on the Dead Sea Scrolls* (1958), Burrows explained how the RSV translators utilized this newly discovered evidence in their work. Burrows brought with him to the 1948 translation-committee meeting a list of the textual variants he had noted in his work in preparation for the publication of the Qumran manuscripts that were assigned to the American Schools of Oriental Research. Of all the variants, thirteen were considered of sufficient importance to result in changes in the translation itself or be included

in textual variants in the footnotes. No variants from the Habakkuk commentary, 1QpHab, were incorporated in the RSV. On later reflection, Burrows (1955:305) concluded, "For myself I must confess that in some cases
where I probably voted for the emendation I am now convinced that our
decision was a mistake, and the Masoretic reading should have been
retained." Although Burrows changed his mind about the value of some
readings, the New Revised Standard Version retained all thirteen items
and added seven more. In *More Light* (1958:146-154), Burrows shares
some of the thinking behind the translators' consideration of 1QIsa^a. By
1964, when Burrows published *Diligently Compared,* a detailed analysis
of the RSV committee's work, he comments on the newer Qumran material not available to the RSV committee, "As they appear [in print] they
will be carefully studied by the Committee to determine their value for
any further revision of R[SV]" (1964: 212).

The policy of the RSV regarding textual notes is explained in the preface:

> The present revision is based on the consonantal Hebrew and Ara-
> maic texts as fixed early in the Christian era and revised by Jewish
> scholars (the "Masoretes") of the sixth to ninth centuries. The vowel
> signs, which were added by the Masoretes, are accepted also in the
> main, but where a more probable and convincing reading can be
> obtained by assuming different vowels, this has been done. No notes
> are given in such cases, because the vowel points are less ancient
> and reliable than the consonants.
>
> Departures from the consonantal text of the best manuscripts have
> been made only where it seems clear that errors in copying had been
> made before the text was standardized. Most of the corrections
> adopted are based on the ancient versions (translations into Greek,
> Aramaic, Syriac, and Latin), which were made before the time of
> the Masoretic revision and therefore reflect earlier forms of the
> text. . . .
>
> Sometimes it is evident that the text has suffered in transmission,
> but none of the versions provides a satisfactory restoration. Here we
> can only follow the best judgment of competent scholars as to the
> most probable reconstruction of the original text. Such corrections
> are indicated in the footnotes by the abbreviation *Cn,* and a transla-
> tion of the Masoretic Text is added. (*Oxford Annotated Bible,* [xii])

When the RSV was first published in 1952 the Dead Sea Scrolls were
not specifically mentioned in either the preface or in the footnotes where
Qumran readings are cited, using instead the general phrase, "One ancient

Ms." This, of course, is not altogether surprising, since the first discoveries were only available during the final phase of the revision process. Also, the diverse nature of the textual witnesses in the Qumran biblical manuscripts was not evident in the Cave 1 Isaiah scrolls. Nevertheless, the RSV was the first major English translation to utilize the Dead Sea Scrolls, a trend that would be greatly expanded in the work of the revisers in the New Revised Standard Version.

The stated policy of the New Revised Standard Version regarding the textual base of their work is in many ways more specific than the statement of the RSV committee. In the preface, "To the Reader," the discovery of additional Dead Sea Scrolls not available to the RSV committee is cited as one of the main contributions to the NRSV. The committee's policy regarding the use and citation of textual evidence begins with a specific statement regarding the edition of the Hebrew Bible they used:

> For the Old Testament the Committee has made use of the *Biblia Hebraica Stuttgartensia* (1977; ed. sec. emendata, 1983). This is an edition of the Hebrew and Aramaic text as current early in the Christian era and fixed by Jewish scholars (the "Masoretes") of the sixth to ninth centuries. The vowel signs, which were added by the Masoretes, are accepted in the main, but where a more probable and convincing reading can be obtained by assuming different vowels, this has been done. No notes are given in such cases, because the vowel points are less ancient and reliable than the consonants. When an alternative reading given by the Masoretes is translated in a footnote, this is identified by the words "Another reading is."
>
> Departures from the consonantal text of the best manuscripts have been made only where it seems clear that errors in copying had been made before the text was standardized. Most of the corrections adopted are based on the ancient versions (translations into Greek, Aramaic, Syriac, and Latin), which were made prior to the time of the work of the Masoretes and which therefore may reflect earlier forms of the Hebrew text. In such instances a footnote specifies the version or versions from which the correction has been derived and also gives a translation of the Masoretic Text. Where it was deemed appropriate to do so, information is supplied in footnotes from subsidiary Jewish traditions concerning other textual readings (the *Tiqqune Sopherim,* "emendations of the scribes"). These are identified in the footnotes as "Ancient Heb tradition."
>
> Occasionally it is evident that the text has suffered in transmission and that none of the versions provides a satisfactory restoration. Here we can only follow the best judgment of competent scholars as to the most probable reconstruction of the original text. Such recon-

structions are indicated in footnotes by the abbreviation Cn ("Correction"), and a translation of the Masoretic Text is added.

The New English Bible (NEB) took a significantly different approach to the text of the Old Testament. A lack of confidence in the Masoretic Text combined with a willingness to make certain textual modifications in pursuit of the "original text" are reflected in the NEB's statement, taken from its preface (first printing):

> The text . . . is not infrequently uncertain and its meaning obscure. . . . The earliest surviving form of the Hebrew text is perhaps that found in the Samaritan Pentateuch. . . . The Hebrew text as thus handed down [by the Massoretes] is full of errors of every kind due to defective archetypes and successive copyists' errors, confusion of letters, omissions and insertions, displacements of words and even whole sentences or paragraphs; and copyists' unhappy attempts to rectify mistakes have only increased the confusion. . . . When the problem before the translators was that of correcting errors in the Hebrew text in order to make sense, they had recourse, first of all, to the ancient versions. . . . These ancient versions, especially when they agree, contribute in varying degrees to the restoration of the Hebrew text when incapable of translation as it stands. . . . In the last resort the scholar may be driven to conjectural emendation of the Hebrew text.

The statement of the Revised English Bible (REB) translators demonstrates a significant shift in their attitude towards the text, when compared with their predecessors:

> It is probable that the Massoretic Text remained substantially unaltered from the second century A.D. to the present time, and this text is reproduced in all Hebrew Bibles. The New English Bible translators used the third edition of Kittel's *Biblia Hebraica.* . . . Despite the care used in the copying of the Massoretic Text, it contains errors, in the correction of which there are witnesses to be heard. None of them is throughout superior to the Massoretic Text, but in particular places their evidence may preserve the correct reading. (xv-xvi)

The *Tanakh,* often called the New Jewish Version (NJV), is a revision of the Jewish translation first published in 1917 under the sponsorship of the Jewish Publication Society of Philadelphia. It is not surprising that the translators state their intention to adhere to the so-called Masoretic Text. (The title pages of the original volumes, published in three parts according to the threefold division of the Hebrew canon, says "according to the Masoretic Text," while the combined one-volume edition says "traditional Hebrew text." Harry Orlinsky objects to *the* Masoretic Text, since there was not a single Masoretic system.) Orlinsky (1917:413) explains the reason for adherence to the traditional text:

> All official translations are meant for the community at large, Protestant, Catholic, or Jewish, as the case may be; they are not meant primarily for scholars, who can control the pertinent data at the source and who are familiar with the canons of textual criticism. The general community has the right to expect the most accurate and intelligible translation possible of the text handed down through the ages. Not only that, once a committee of translators begins to resort to emendation, it is difficult to draw the line.

Following Orlinsky's principles, the committee undertook faithfully to follow the traditional (Masoretic) text. There were certain points, however, at which footnotes appeared necessary—that is, "where textual variants are to be found in some of the ancient manuscripts or versions of the Bible" (preface to *The Torah*).

The New American Bible offers another approach to textual considerations. As an official Roman Catholic translation, one significant difference from Protestant-sponsored translations is the inclusion of the books of the Deuterocanon interspersed among the books of the Protocanon. Traditionally, certain evidence from the ancient versions is held in high regard as textual witnesses. More importantly for our present study, the NAB had extensive access to Qumran evidence. The stated perspective of the NAB is:

> Where the translation supposes the received text—Hebrew, Aramaic, or Greek, as the case may be—ordinarily contained in the best-known editions, as the original or the oldest extant form, no additional remarks are necessary. But for those who are happily able to study the original text of the Scripture at firsthand, a supplementary series of textual notes pertaining to the Old Testament is added in an appendix to the typical edition published by the St. Anthony Guild Press. These furnish a guide in those cases in which the editorial board judges that the manuscripts in the original languages, or the evidence of the ancient versions, or some similar source, furnish the correct reading of a passage, or at least a reading more true to the original than that customarily printed in the available editions.
> The Massoretic text of 1 and 2 Samuel has in numerous instances

been corrected by the more ancient manuscripts Samuel a, b, and c from Cave 4 of Qumran, with the aid of important evidence from the Septuagint in both its oldest form and its Lucianic recension. . . .

The basic text for the Psalms in the first edition is not the Massoretic but one which the editors considered closer to the original inspired form, namely the Hebrew text underlying the new Latin Psalter of the Church, the *Liber Psalmorum* (1944, 1945). Nevertheless, they retained full liberty to establish the reading of the original text on sound critical principles. (preface, v)

A revised edition of the Psalms was published in 1992. In the new edition, Qumran evidence is added in support of fifteen textual variants already followed in the first edition, and an additional three variants are followed based on the Qumran evidence.

The conservative theological stance of the translators of the New International Version (NIV) is reflected in their prefatory statement:

For the Old Testament the standard Hebrew text, The Masoretic Text as published in the latest editions of *Biblia Hebraica,* was used throughout. The Dead Sea Scrolls contain material bearing on an earlier stage of the Hebrew text. They were consulted, as were the Samaritan Pentateuch and the ancient scribal traditions relating to textual changes. Sometimes a variant Hebrew reading in the margin of the Masoretic Text was followed instead of the text itself. Such instances, being variants within the Masoretic tradition, are not specified by footnotes. In rare cases, words in the consonantal text were divided differently from the way they appear in the Masoretic Text. Footnotes indicate this. The translators also consulted the more important early versions—the Septuagint; Aquila, Symmachus, and Theodotion; the Vulgate; the Syriac Peshitta; the Targums; and for the Psalms the *Juxta Hebraica* of Jerome. Readings from these versions were occasionally followed where the Masoretic Text seemed doubtful and where accepted principles of textual criticism showed that one or more of these textual witnesses appeared to provide the correct reading. Such instances are footnoted. Sometimes vowel letters and vowel signs did not, in the judgment of the translators, represent the correct vowels for the original consonantal text. Accordingly some words were read with a different set of vowels. These instances are usually not indicated in footnotes.

For the Good News Bible (GNB):

The basic text for the Old Testament is the Masoretic Text printed in *Biblia Hebraica* (third edition, 1937), edited by Rudolph Kittel. In some instances the words of the printed consonantal text have been divided differently or have been read with a different set of vowels; at times a variant reading (*qere*) in the margin of the Hebrew text has been followed instead of the reading in the text (*kethib*); and in other instances a variant reading supported by one or more Hebrew manuscripts has been adopted. Where no Hebrew source yields a satisfactory meaning in the context, the translation has either followed one or more of the ancient versions (Greek, Syriac, Latin) or has adopted a reconstructed text (technically referred to as a conjectural emendation) based on scholarly agreement; such departures from the Hebrew are indicated in footnotes. (preface)

After completing our book-by-book survey we will better be able to judge how faithful these translations have been to their stated principles and whether they made good use of the evidence of the manuscripts from the Dead Sea.

Several recent translations that are not regularly included in this study are, nevertheless, of interest because of their general policy regarding the textual basis of the Old Testament.

The New King James Version (NKJV) of 1982 is noted for its belief that the textual basis of the KJV in the New Testament, namely the Textus Receptus, should be retained, with certain adjustments to the Byzantine or Majority text. For the Old Testament the basic text was *Biblia Hebraica Stuttgartensia,* whose consonantal text differs very little from the Hebrew Bible text used for the KJV. According to the preface (vi), "the NKJV draws on the resources of relevant manuscripts from the Dead Sea caves." However, evidence from the Dead Sea Scrolls is cited in only six footnotes in the entire Old Testament, and only in Isaiah 49:5 is the Dead Sea Scroll reading followed in the text, where it is cited in support of the *qere* reading of the Masoretic Text. The six references are: Deuteronomy 32:43; 1 Samuel 1:24; Isaiah 10:16; 22:8; 38:14; 49:5. In Isaiah 38:14 the NKJV renders LORD without citing any textual evidence, against Lord (for Hebrew *adonai*) as found in the Masoretic Text and 1QIsa[a]. The same textual evidence prevails in verse 16, where NKJV again translates LORD, but without any textual note. Despite the implication of the preface, the NKJV has made only limited use of the Dead Sea Scrolls.

The New Jerusalem Bible (NJB), which is the 1985 revision of the Jerusalem Bible, says, "For the Old Testament the Masoretic Text is used. . . . Only when this text presents insuperable difficulties have emendations or the versions or other Hebrew manuscripts or the ancient versions (notably the LXX and Syriac) been used" (xii).

Die Gute Nachricht (1982), the common-language German version, strove to follow the Masoretic Text as much as possible. The translators took advantage of recent discoveries, including Qumran, which helped to reshape the understanding of the history of the Old Testament text. The translators gave careful consideration to the text-critical analysis of the Hebrew Old Testament Text Project. In the Appendix (1982:300) the translators explain that the basis of their textual decisions was HOTTP. They departed from the Masoretic Text only when there were good reasons for doing so. They recognized the importance of the well-established Hebrew Old Testament text of A.D. 100.

Traduction Oecuménique de la Bible (TOB), a modern-language French translation, was diligent in following the Masoretic Text as much as possible, not as a reversion to a non-critical approach to the text of the Old Testament but in recognition of their understanding of the textual situation at stage two in the development of the text, as set forth by the Hebrew Old Testament Text Project. In their preface the translators explain that the *traditional text* (i.e., the Masoretic Text) is the basis of their work, yet they noted any place where they did not follow this text. They point out that in the present state of the scientific study of the Old Testament text, this official text of Judaism is the only text that is firmly established. The text also serves as a common basis for an "ecumenical" translation.

Die Gute Nachricht and *Traduction Oecuménique de la Bible* are two major recent translations that have consciously striven to follow the Masoretic Text as closely as possible, basing their view on recent manuscript discoveries (especially at Qumran) and on the principles established in the HOTTP committee. Of all the recent translations of the last decade, *Traduction Oecuménique de la Bible* deviates least from the Masoretic Text—with the possible exception of the Jewish Publication Society translation in English.

Before examining individual passages affected by Dead Sea Scroll discoveries in these modern Old Testament translations, it is important to survey the scope of the biblical manuscripts found at Qumran and at nearby Dead Sea locations. A survey of the manuscript-by-manuscript description given in the next chapter shows that there are only about a dozen manuscripts which preserve large sections of the biblical books. But the limited

STAGES IN OLD TESTAMENT TEXTUAL TRANSMISSION

HOTTP	HUBP	WALTKE
(1) **Ur-text:** recoverable primarily through literary criticism, archaeology, and philology	(1) First stage: (proto-biblical) "ends before the start of all ms documentation. Reconstruction of the Ur-text is not the supreme goal."	(1) **Composition** (to 400 B.C.) Double tendency: centrifugal and centripetal
(2) **Accepted Text:** in forms accepted by various communities (to A.D. 70)	(2) extra-Masoretic 300 B.C. and	(2) **Preservation** (e.g., IQIsa[b]) **Revision:** three recensions and one mixed type developed
3) **Received Text** standardized by canon formation (= proto-MT)	(3) proto-Masoretic final stages of individual model manuscripts	(3) **Standardization:** A.D. 70–1000
(4) **Masoretic Text**	(4) **Masoretic text**	
See Barthélemy: 1976	*See Goshen-Gottstein:1967*	*See Waltke: 1976*

TALMON	SARNA	BARR
(1) **Oral Phase** to mid-sixth century "No longer possible to reconstruct the textual evolution . . ."	(1) **The Earliest Period** to 300 B.C.	(1) **Greek Translations** "little conscious striving to use constant equivalences"
(2) **Written Transmission**	(2) Starting point of period two is determined by the fortuitous existence of manuscript documentation	(2) "an increasing desire for accuracy which it was thought would be attained through increased regularity in the equivalences used"
(3) **Stage Three** "the pivot around which any investigation into the history of the Bible text turns, . . . progressive demarcation of books accepted as scripture."	(3) **Third Period** First century A.D. to ninth century	(3) "imitative style of translation . . . found, above all, in Aquila"
	(4) The major codexes: B19[a], Aleppo, etc.	(4) "a positive preference for variety" (Jerome)
See Talmon: 1970	*See Sarna: 1972*	*See Barr: 1979*

evidence gleaned from the hundreds of poorly preserved manuscripts provides another dimension to the picture.

Scholars now recognize that the type of text found in the Masoretic Text was very persistent and stable, especially as compared to various recensions that fluctuated in their adherence to two types of text: (1) the Hebrew text on which the Old Greek translations were based, and (2) the Samaritan Pentateuch. Initially there was a tendency for scholars to characterize the Qumran biblical manuscripts as belonging to one of the three text types isolated in earlier Old Testament textual studies. Closer analysis now indicates that many of these manuscripts should not be pigeon-holed into existing categories. Bible translators need to weigh textual evidence in light of this interplay between unity and diversity of textual witnesses.

PART TWO
DESCRIPTION OF OLD TESTAMENT MANUSCRIPTS

Most of the biblical manuscripts discovered in the area of the Dead Sea since the late 1940s have now been published. Nine of the eleven caves at Qumran have yielded at least some biblical manuscripts. Caves 1, 4, and 11 have yielded the most important finds, both in quantity and in textual variety. Official publication of the Qumran manuscripts have appeared primarily in the series entitled Discoveries in the Judean Desert. Volumes 3, 4, and 5 of the nine published volumes (through 1992) bear the series title Discoveries in the Judean Desert of Jordan—reflecting the political situation in the region at that time. Definitive publication of the earliest Qumran Cave 1 discoveries, as well as two important manuscripts from Qumran Cave 11, have also been published outside the Discoveries in the Judean Desert series. The Cave 1 manuscripts obtained by Israel include 1QIsa^b.

Most of the biblical manuscripts from Qumran Cave 4 have not been published in an official edition. However, the contents of the vast majority of these scrolls have been made known to the academic community in journal articles, dissertations, or elsewhere. A problem facing those who want to study the manuscripts is the fact that in some cases the publications do not give the actual text in its entirety, but only the variant readings that were considered significant by the author. Several recently published bibliographic guides provide a convenient guide to the relevant publications. These include Joseph A. Fitzmyer, *The Dead Sea Scrolls: Major Publications and Tools for Study,* revised edition (Atlanta: Scholars Press, 1990). Eugene Ulrich's article in *Revue de Qumrân* 14 (1989:207-228), "The Biblical Scrolls from Qumran Cave 4: A Progress Report of Their Publication," provides a comprehensive list of all known biblical manuscripts found in Cave 4.

The Ancient Biblical Manuscript Center (ABMC) in Claremont, California is an official depository site for photographs of the Dead Sea Scrolls. Stephen Reed of ABMC has published *Dead Sea Scrolls Inventory Proj-*

ect: Lists of Documents, Photographs and Museum Plates (1991-1992) in twelve fascicles:

1. Qumran Cave 1
2. Qumran Minor Caves
3. Murabba'at
4. Qumran Cave 4Q128-4Q186
5. Qumran Cave 4Q482-4Q520
6. 11Q
7. Qumran Cave 4 (4Q1-127) Biblical
8. Qumran Cave 4 (4Q521-4Q575) Starcky
9. Qumran Cave 4 (4Q364-4Q481) Strugnell
10. Qumran Cave 4 (4Q196-4Q363) Milik
11. Khirbet Mird
12. Wadi ed Daliyeh

FASCICLES IN CAVE NUMBER ORDER

Qumran Cave 1: Fascicle 1
Qumran Cave 2: Fascicle 2
Qumran Cave 3: Fascicle 2
Qumran Cave 4:
> 4Q1-127: Fascicle 7
> 4Q128-186: Fascicle 4
> 4Q187-195: (no information available)
> 4Q196-363: Fascicle 10
> 4Q364-481: Fascicle 9
> 4Q482-520: Fascicle 5
> 4Q521-575: Fascicle 8

Qumran Cave 5: Fascicle 2
Qumran Cave 6: Fascicle 2
Qumran Cave 7: Fascicle 2
Qumran Cave 8: Fascicle 2
Qumran Cave 9: Fascicle 2 (one papyrus fragment only)
Qumran Cave 10: Fascicle 2 (one ostracon only)
Qumran Cave 11: Fascicle 6

Khirbet Mird: Fascicle 11 (including NT Greek and Christian
   Palestinian Aramaic MSS)
Masada: Fascicle 14
Murabba'at: Fascicle 3
Nahal Hever: Fascicle 13
Wadi ed Daliyeh: Fascicle 12 (deeds, bullae, coins, and rings)
Wadi Seiyal: Fascicle 13

Each fascicle lists the manuscripts in document order and also gives the corresponding number of the photograph. Reed's *Inventory* is especially important for the material that has not as yet been published. Fascicle 7 details the biblical manuscripts found in Cave 4 and is of particular interest to us. The documentation of the other unpublished Cave 4 material will also provide an important guide for researchers interested in the non-biblical texts.

OFFICIAL PUBLICATIONS
BY CLARENDON PRESS, OXFORD, IN THE DISCOVERIES IN THE JUDEAN DESERT (OF JORDAN) (DJD) SERIES:

DJD 1: *Qumran Cave 1*

DJD 2: *Les grottes de Murabba'at*

DJD 3: *Les 'petites grottes' de Qumrân* (2Q, 3Q, 5Q, 6Q, 7Q, 8Q, 9Q, and 10Q)
All the manuscripts found in Cave 7 are in Greek, written on papyrus. Only one tiny scrap was found in each of caves 9 and 10.

DJD 4: *The Psalms Scroll of Qumran Cave 11*. 1965.
Sanders's later edition, *The Dead Sea Psalms Scroll* (Ithica, New York: Cornell U. Press, 1967), also contains "Fragment E," identified as part of 11QPs^a only after the publication of DJD 4.

DJD 5: *Qumrân grotte 4. I (4Q158-4Q186)*.
No biblical texts, but thirteen biblical commentaries and several biblical paraphrases are included in this volume.

DJD 6: *Qumrân grotte 4. II (4Q128-4Q157)*.
This collection includes phylacteries, mezuzot, and two Targum (Aramaic translations of the Hebrew Bible) manuscripts.

DJD 7: *Qumrân grotte 4. III (4Q482-4Q520)*.
No biblical texts; a few fragments from Jubilees and the Testament of Judah.

DJD 8: *The Greek Minor Prophets Scroll from Nahal Hever (8HevXIIgr)*.

DJD 9: *Qumran Cave Four: Vol. 4. Paleo-Hebrew and Greek Biblical Manuscripts*.

By the American Schools of Oriental Research:

The Dead Sea Scrolls of St. Mark's Monastery, Volume I: *The Isaiah Manuscript [1QIsa^a] and the Habakkuk Commentary [1QpHab]* (New Haven, 1950).

These scrolls were republished with reproductions of John C. Trever's original color photographs (Jerusalem: The Albright Institute of Archaeological Research and The Shrine of the Book, 1972). They were rephotographed under the direction of E. Qimron and published in *The Dead Sea Scrolls,* M. Sekine, editor [text in Japanese] (Tokyo: Kodansha, 1979).

The Paleo-Hebrew Leviticus Scroll (11QpaleoLev), D. N. Freedman and K. A. Mathews, editors. (Winona Lake, IN: Eisenbrauns for the American Schools of Oriental Research, 1985).

By the Hebrew University, Jerusalem:

The Dead Sea Scrolls of the Hebrew University [including 1QIsa[b]]. (Jerusalem: Magnes Press, 1955).

By the Royal Dutch Academy of Sciences, who purchased the publication rights to a group of scrolls from Cave 11:

Le Targum de Job de la grotte XI de Qumrân [11QtgJob], J. P. M. van der Ploeg and A. S. van der Woude, editors (Leiden: E. J. Brill, 1971).

MAJOR PRELIMINARY EDITIONS

Ulrich, Eugene C. "Daniel Manuscripts from Qumran [4QDan[a,b,c]]," BASOR 286 (1987:17-36) and 274 (1989:3-26). Includes plates, transcription, and discussion of the texts.

Many other individual manuscripts have received preliminary publication in journal articles and other scholarly works. At times these works may include complete transcriptions with plates. Relevant bibliography will be given under the specific manuscript.

OTHER EDITIONS

By the Biblical Archaeological Society:

A Facsimile Edition of the Dead Sea Scrolls, Robert H. Eisenman and James M. Robinson, editors. (Washington, D.C.: Biblical Archaeology Society, 1991).

DIRECTORY OF THE MANUSCRIPTS

The following directory lists all of the known manuscripts found in the area of the Dead Sea, both from Qumran and other sources in the area. It is still possible that in the myriad of fragments housed in the Rockefeller Museum and in the many published photographs something will be discovered that contains biblical text, although it would be quite fragmentary. Rumors still persist that other major manuscripts have been withheld from view. This possibility seems quite unlikely, especially for biblical texts.

Another factor affecting the enumeration of Qumran manuscripts is the determination by scholars working on the texts that a manuscript formerly thought to be written by only one scribe actually represents two or more different manuscripts. This reevaluation has, for example, resulted in the identification of three different copies of Jeremiah formerly considered to be 4QJer[b].

The entries for each manuscript are divided into a maximum of five sections. In cases where the manuscripts have not yet received scholarly evaluation, relevant information is not available. In these cases, we have written *uncertain.*

Name: lists the manuscript according to the system devised during the early stages of publication. Qumran manuscripts are designated Q, preceded by the number of the cave in which the manuscript was discovered. The caves are numbered chronologically by order of discovery, not by geographic relationship. Except for the first major scrolls discovered, each manuscript has been numbered according to the following sequence: (1) biblical manuscripts in the order of the Hebrew canon; (2) manuscripts with biblical content such as phylacteries and commentaries (*pesharim*); and (3) all other manuscripts. For Cave 4 the numbers are assigned in blocks of manuscripts as initially assigned to the editing committee.

Each manuscript is also usually given an abbreviation based on its content. For the biblical manuscripts these abbreviations are quite evident. For documents that were unknown before their discovery at Qumran these abbreviations are sometimes rather cryptic, especially to the uninformed. Where manuscripts have been published using the number system as well as the book abbreviation, the manuscript number is given in parentheses.

Other abbreviations used in the manuscript designations:

superscript letters = (as in 1QIsa^{a,b,c}) designate different manuscripts of the same biblical book. The sequence of letters have
been assigned in the order of identification, not book content.
gk/Gk = Greek Old Testament manuscripts
p = *pesher* (meaning "interpretation"), a commentary on a biblical
book
paleo = Hebrew manuscripts written in archaic Hebrew orthography
pap = manuscript written on papyrus (all other manuscripts are on
parchment)
par = paraphrase
tg = Aramaic Targums

Content: lists the contents of the manuscript. It must be kept in mind
that in many cases the manuscript is very fragmentary and may only
contain a few words, or even a few letters. In the chart of biblical manuscripts (pp. 87-103), verses extant for only a word or less are designated
by {O}. While the occurrence of so little information may seem to be
inconsequential, it may provide useful clues. For example, the existence
of only a letter or two on the last line of a fragment can indicate that a
particular clause is included (or not present) in the manuscript, while the
opposite may be true in other manuscripts. Also, if the fragment can be
located in relation to the margin, and the average line length can be
determined (as is frequently the case), the textual critic can often determine with a fair degree of certainty what could or could not fit into the
space before the tiny fragment. In cases where a manuscript has been
studied, but only variants given, it may not be possible to determine
where the extant text begins and ends in individual verses. These verses
are marked with a ♦ in the index of Old Testament manuscripts (pp. 141-
168). In the comments below, a question mark (?) immediately follows
any verse that is questionable. The designation (=) in biblical citations
provides equivalent English Bible versification.

Bibliography: provides only a brief guide to the manuscript. All of the
biblical manuscripts except those found in Cave 4 have received official publication. The bibliography gives the volume number in the Discoveries in the Judean Desert series or other official publication (see
pp. 43-44). These publications always include a complete transcription,
photographs, and a full discussion of the characteristics of the manuscripts considered. In a few cases, publication of additional discoveries

or significant reevaluations are also given in the bibliography (for an example, see 11QPs^a).

In the case of Cave 4 manuscripts that await official publication, the following information is given: Plate number(s) from the Eisenman and Robinson (1991) edition (designated ER), followed by the Palestine Archaeological Museum (PAM) number. Generally, only the major plates are listed. Other fragments, sometimes scattered over numerous plates, are not listed here, but their existence is noted by a + following the list of plate numbers. A full list of plates can be found in Reed (1991–1992). Next are given references to major treatments that may contain the full text or a thorough evaluation of textual variants, as well as photographs. A large number of Cave 4 manuscripts have been treated extensively in a series of recent Harvard University doctoral dissertations. These dissertations are listed here and in the bibliography, although they may not be readily available.

Date: provides an approximation of the time when the manuscript was copied. This information is generally derived from official or preliminary official publications. As might be expected, dissenting opinions have been offered by various scholars. However, there is little doubt that the Qumran manuscripts were written no earlier than about 250 B.C. and no later than A.D. 75. Recent paleographic studies (see especially Tov [1986]) have demonstrated that not all of the manuscripts were written at Qumran.

The dating of biblical manuscripts is crucial for their proper evaluation and consequent determination of the worth for textual criticism. One factor for determining the age of manuscripts is the archaeological environment in which they were found. For example, at Qumran there is evidence of an earthquake in 31 B.C. that resulted in the temporary abandonment of the community until it was rebuilt about the turn of the era. About seventy years later (in A.D.70) Qumran was destroyed during the Jewish war and Roman invasion. Apparently a small garrison occupied Masada for several years until this fort fell. This archaeological history of the community seems to be confirmed by the coins found at the site (de Vaux, 1978:978-986). Although de Vaux's archaeological work has been criticized by some, the general reconstruction of the history of the community has been established.

In any event, the evidence of the biblical manuscripts for the history of the textual transmission of the Hebrew Bible remains important and would be little affected by minor adjustments in chronology. Assuming that the Dead Sea Scrolls found near the Qumran settlement were the product of that community, then the latest date for the manuscripts hidden in nearby caves is about A.D. 70. Although some scholars still question the connection of the Qumran community with the caves (for example, Golb [1980]), most agree that the connection is firmly established and the manuscripts can safely be assumed to have been written no later than the middle of the first century A.D. Even if the connection of the manuscripts with the Qumran community is accepted, there is paleographic and orthographic evidence that some of the manuscripts, including biblical texts, were brought to Qumran from the outside (Tov:1986). For example, Tov believes that all the biblical manuscripts written in paleo-Hebrew characters were brought in from the outside. The scrolls written at Qumran in Qumran orthography reflect a freer attitude to the text, using fuller spelling through the use of more vowel letters and introducing some new grammatical forms (1986:42-43).

The paleographic dating of the manuscripts in this catalog follows a chronological frame of reference such as Hasmonean or Herodian, and a stylistic description—formal, semi-formal, semi-cursive, cursive. The categorizations are as follows:

> Proto-Jewish Scripts (developed from early Aramaic): from the mid-third century B.C. to 175 B.C.
> Early Hasmonean: c. 175–125 B.C.
> Hasmonean: c. 125–100 B.C.
> Late Hasmonean: c. 100–30 B.C.
> Early Herodian: c. 30–25 B.C.
> Herodian: c. 25 B.C.–A.D. 50
> Late Herodian: c. A.D. 50–70
> Post Herodian: c. A.D. 70

For further details on paleographic study as applied to the Qumran manuscripts, see part 1, pages 12-15. If the date is not given for a particular manuscript, it can be assumed that it is dated between 250 B.C. and A.D. 70.

Significance: describes both the textual character of the manuscript and its general significance to translation. Specific implications for translation are discussed in part 3. When this entry does not accompany a manuscript listed below, the reader can assume there was nothing significant to say about the text of that manuscript.

THE MANUSCRIPTS
QUMRAN CAVE 1

Name: 1QGen (= 1Q1)
Content: Genesis 1:18-21; 3:11-14; 22:13-15; 23:17-19; 24:22-24
Bibliography: DJD 1
Date: First century B.C.

Name: 1QExod (= 1Q2)
Content: Exodus 16:12-16; 19:24-25; 20:1, 25-26; 21:1, 4-5
Bibliography: DJD 1
Date: First century B.C.

Name: 1QpaleoLev(+Num) (= 1Q3)
Content: Leviticus 11:10-11; 19:30-34; 20:20-24; 21:24; 22:2-6; 23:4-8; other scattered fragments
Bibliography: DJD 1; McLean (1982) distinguishes three different manuscripts, which he designates 1QpaleoLev^a, 1QpaleoLev^b, and 1QpaleoNum.
Date: Birnbaum (1950:27) estimates that this manuscript may be as old as the second half of the fifth century B.C., but this paleo-Hebrew hand is difficult to date, since the scribe was consciously imitating an older style of writing. Hanson (1964:41) proposes a date somewhere between 125 and 75 B.C.

Name: 1Qpaleo(Lev+)Num (= 1Q3)
Content: Numbers 1:48-50; other scattered fragments possibly from chapters 27 and 36
Bibliography: DJD 1; McLean (1982)
Date: (See preceding reference)

Name: 1QDeut^a (= 1Q4)
Content: Deuteronomy 1:22-25; 4:47-49; 8:18-19; 9:27-28; 11:27-30; 13:1-6, 13-14; 14:21, 24-25; 16:4, 6-7
Bibliography: DJD 1
Date: First century B.C.

Name: 1QDeut^b (= 1Q5)
Content: Deuteronomy 1:9-13; 8:8-9; 9:10; 11:30-31; 17:16; 21:8-9; 24:10-16; 25:13-18; 28:44-48; 29:9-20; 30:19-20; 31:1-10, 12-13; 32:17-29; 33:12-24
Bibliography: DJD 1
Date: First century B.C.

Name: 1QJudg (= 1Q6)
Content: Judges 6:20-22; 8:1(?); 9:2-6, 28-31, 40-43, 48-49

Bibliography: DJD 1
Date: First century B.C.
Significance: Based on line-length considerations, the phrase "and Abime-lech remained at Arumah" in the MT (Judges 9:41) was probably miss-ing in this manuscript.

Name: 1QSam (= 1Q7)
Content: 1 Samuel 18:17-18; 2 Samuel 20:6-10; 21:16-18; 23:9-12
Bibliography: DJD 1
Date: First century B.C.
Significance: Several proper names are spelled the same as in Chronicles.

Name: 1QPs^a (= 1Q10)
Content: Psalms 86:5-8; 92:12-14; 94:16; 95:11–96:2; 119:31-34, 43-48, 77-79
Bibliography: DJD 1
Date: First century B.C.

Name: 1QPs^b (= 1Q11)
Content: Psalms 126:6; 127:1-5; 128:3
Bibliography: DJD 1
Date: First century B.C.
Significance: The tetragrammaton (i.e., four letters written as YHWH to represent Yahweh) is written in paleo-Hebrew letters. There are a few orthographic variants from proto-MT.

Name: 1QPs^c (= 1Q12)
Content: Psalm 44:3-5, 7, 9, 23-25
Bibliography: DJD 1
Date: First century B.C.
Significance: The manuscript is quite fragmentary, but it appears to fol-low the full orthography typical of Qumran manuscripts.

Name: 1QIsa^a
Content: Isaiah 1:1-31; 2:1-22; 3–4 complete; 5:1-30; 6:1-13; 7:1-25; 8:1-23; 9:1-20; 10:1-34; 11–44 complete; 45:1-25; 46–65 complete; 66:1-24
Bibliography: Burrows (1950), Trever (1972)
Date: c. 100 B.C.
Significance: The text is generally similar to proto-MT, but with some significant variants. Many of these variants are in orthography, with a strong preference for *plene* (full) spellings. This characteristic has led to the belief that this scroll was a "popular" copy because the *plene* spelling makes reading easier. This was the first Dead Sea Scroll to receive widespread attention. The RSV committee, which was nearing completion of their work at the time, adopted thirteen readings from 1QIsa^a.

Name: 1QIsa^b (includes 1Q8)
Content: Isaiah 7:22-25; 8:1; 10:17-19; 12:3-6; 13:1-8, 16-19; 15:3-9; 16:1-

2, 7-11; 19:7-17, 20-25; 20:1; 22:11-18, 24-25; 23:1-4; 24:18-23; 25:1-8;
26:1-5; 28:15-20; 29:1-8; 30:10-14, 21-26; 35:4-5; 37:8-12; 38:12-22; 39:1-
8; 40:2-3; 41:3-23; 43:1-13, 23-27; 44:21-28; 45:1-13; 46:3-13; 47:1-14;
48:17-22; 49:1-15; 50:7-11; 51:1-10; 52:7-15; 53:1-12; 54:1-6; 55:2-13;
56:1-12; 57:1-4, 17-21; 58:1-14; 59:1-8, 20-21; 60:1-22; 61:1-2;
62:2-12; 63:1-19; 64:1, 6-8; 65:17-25; 66:1-24
Bibliography: Sukenik (1955); additional fragments in DJD 1
Date: Herodian
Significance: The text is quite close to proto-MT. Rarely utilized for support of variant readings, but it confirms the existence of a stable proto-
MT text type.

Name: 1QEzek (= 1Q9)
Content: Ezekiel 4:16-17; 5:1
Bibliography: DJD 1
Date: First century B.C.
Significance: Preserves only about eight words. A larger space in the
manuscript at the end of Ezekiel 4:17 corresponds to a *petuhah* (an
"open" paragraph marker) found in the MT.

Name: 1QDan^a (= 1Q71)
Content: Daniel 1:10-17; 2:2-6
Bibliography: Trever (1965)
Date: c. A.D. 70

Name: 1QDan^b (= 1Q72)
Content: Daniel 3:22-30
Bibliography: Trever (1965)
Date: Herodian
Significance: On the basis of paleography, Trever (1970) considers this
the latest Qumran manuscript.

QUMRAN CAVE 2

Name: 2QGen (= 2Q1)
Content: Genesis 19:27-28; 36:6, 35-37
Bibliography: DJD 3
Date: Herodian
Significance: The two small fragments show no divergencies from the MT.

Name: 2QExod^a (= 2Q2)
Content: Exodus 1:11-14; 7:1-4; 9:27-29; 11:3-7; 12:32-41; 21:18-20(?);
26:11-13; 30:21(?), 23-25; 32:32-34
Bibliography: DJD 3
Date: Herodian period
Significance: Contains several readings supported by the LXX.

Name: 2QExod^b (= 2Q3)
Content: Exodus 4:31; 12:26-27(?); 18:21-22; 19:9; 21:37; 22:1-2, 15-19;
27:17-19; 31:16-17; 34:10

Bibliography: DJD 3

Date: Herodian

Significance: Uses *plene* spelling; the tetragrammaton is written in paleo-Hebrew script. The text differs from proto-MT in several morphological details and finds occasional support in the ancient versions.

Name: 2QExod^c^ (= 2Q4)

Content: Exodus 5:3-5

Bibliography: DJD 3

Date: uncertain

Significance: The fragment contains only three words, each at the beginning of a new line.

Name: 2QpaleoLev (= 2Q5)

Content: Leviticus 11:22-29

Bibliography: DJD 3

Date: First century B.C.

Significance: Uses *plene* spelling; verses 25-26 agree with several LXX MSS and the Samaritan Pentateuch.

Name: 2QNum^a^ (= 2Q6)

Content: Numbers 3:38-41, 51; 4:1-3

Bibliography: DJD 3

Date: Herodian

Significance: Fragment one contains only the opening letters of each of ten lines. On the basis of line-length considerations, there may have been a textual variant in verse 39 relating to "and Aaron," which is marked in the MT with *puncta extraordinaria,* a series of dots the Masoretes wrote above the letter to mark a word about which there were textual or doctrinal reservations. The word is lacking in the Samaritan Pentateuch and Syriac. Unfortunately, we cannot be certain that it was missing here as well.

Name: 2QNum^b^ (= 2Q7)

Content: Numbers 33:47-53

Bibliography: DJD 3

Date: early Herodian

Significance: Some spellings support the pronunciation known from the Samaritan Pentateuch, but there are no significant textual variants.

Name: 2QNum^c^ (= 2Q8)

Content: Numbers 7:88

Bibliography: DJD 3

Date: Herodian

Significance: The single fragment preserves only four words.

Name: 2QNum^d?^ (= 2Q9) [may be part of 2QNum^b^]

Content: Numbers 18:8-9

Bibliography: DJD 3

Date: uncertain
Significance: The fragment preserves parts of only six words.

Name: 2QDeut^a (= 2Q10)
Content: Deuteronomy 1:7-9
Bibliography: DJD 3
Date: First century B.C.
Significance: There are only small fragments of four lines. There are no notable textual characteristics.

Name: 2QDeut^b (= 2Q11)
Content: Deuteronomy 17:12-15
Bibliography: DJD 3
Date: Herodian
Significance: The manuscript was written in full (*plene*) orthography, typical of the manuscripts of the Qumran community.

Name: 2QDeut^c (= 2Q12)
Content: Deuteronomy 10:8-12
Bibliography: DJD 3
Date: Herodian
Significance: Written in full orthography, the manuscript often agrees with the LXX.

Name: 2QRuth^a (= 2Q16)
Content: Ruth 2:13-23; 3:1-8; 4:3-4
Bibliography: DJD 3
Date: First half of the first century A.D.
Significance: The text generally agrees with the MT. Supports the *qere* (i.e., the marginal reading in the MT) of Ruth 3:3.

Name: 2QRuth^b (= 2Q17)
Content: Ruth 3:13-18
Bibliography: DJD 3
Date: c. 50 B.C.
Significance: The text and orthography generally agree with the MT.

Name: 2QJob (= 2Q15)
Content: Job 33:28-30
Bibliography: DJD 3
Date: Herodian
Significance: The remnants of the four or five words in this small fragment agree with the MT.

Name: 2QPs (= 2Q14)
Content: Psalms 103:2-11; 104:6-11
Bibliography: DJD 3
Date: Herodian

Significance: The text of fragment one, which contains the opening lines of Psalm 103, is written in red.

Name: 2QJer (= 2Q13)
Content: Jeremiah 42:7-11, 14; 43:8-11; 44:1-3, 12-14; 46:27-28; 47:1-7; 48:7, 25-39, 43-45; 49:10
Bibliography: DJD 3
Date: Herodian
Significance: Although some readings agree with the LXX, the order of the chapters follows the proto-MT. The differences between the MT and LXX of Jeremiah are significant and extensive. Overall, the LXX is one-eighth shorter than the MT and the arrangement of chapters is different. See the 4QJer manuscripts for additional evidence.

QUMRAN CAVE 3

Name: 3QPs (= 3Q2)
Content: Psalm 2:6-7
Bibliography: DJD 3
Date: First century A.D.
Significance: Since it preserves only five words, it is too fragmentary to characterize.

Name: 3QLam (= 3Q3)
Content: Lamentations 1:10-12; 3:53-62
Bibliography: DJD 3
Date: Herodian
Significance: The tetragrammaton is written in paleo-Hebrew script. Although quite fragmentary, the spaces available in the lacunae are consistent with the MT.

Name: 3QEzek (= 3Q1)
Content: Ezekiel 16:31-33
Bibliography: DJD 3
Date: Herodian
Significance: It is quite fragmentary—only eleven letters are preserved.

QUMRAN CAVE 4

Name: 4QGen(+Exod)[a]
Content: portions of Genesis chapters 22, 27, 34–37, 39–40, 45–49
Bibliography: plates: Genesis: ER 658 (42.151), 1093 (43.009); Exodus: ER 665 (42.158), 1090 (43.006) +, 1094 (43.010); Davila (1988, 1991, forthcoming)
Date: c. 125–100 B.C.

Name: 4QGen[b]
Content: Genesis 1:1-27; 2:14-19; 4:2-4; 5:13 or 14
Bibliography: plate: ER 1088 (43.004); Davila (1990, forthcoming)
Date: A.D. 50–68 or possibly later

Significance: The text is proto-MT, except for one orthographic variant (Davila: forthcoming).

Name: 4QGen^c
Content: portions of Genesis 40 and 41
Bibliography: plates: ER 1622 (43.698), 1721 (44.016); Davila (1988, 1990, forthcoming)
Date: Herodian
Significance: The manuscript is very fragmentary and poorly preserved, although it usually agrees with the MT.

Name: 4QGen^d
Content: Genesis 1:18-27
Bibliography: plates: ER 662 (42.155), 974 (42.725); Davila (1988, 1990, forthcoming)
Date: c. 50–25 B.C., late Hasmonean formal handwriting
Significance: The text is proto-MT except for orthographic variants. The manuscript is very fragmentary and poorly preserved (Davila 1990).

Name: 4QGen^e
Content: portions of Genesis 36–37, 40–43, 49
Bibliography: plate: ER 1089 (43.005); Davila (1988, 1990, forthcoming)
Date: late Hasmonean to early Herodian

Name: 4QGen^f
Content: Genesis 48:1-11
Bibliography: plate: ER 976 (42.727); Davila (1988)
Date: late Hasmonean

Name: 4QGen^g
Content: Genesis 1:1-11, 13-22; 2:6-7 or 18-19
Bibliography: plate: ER 972 (42.723); Davila (1990, forthcoming)
Date: late Hasmonean
Significance: The manuscript has a number of interesting variants from proto-MT (Davila 1990).

Name: 4QGen$^{h\ h(1),\ h(2)\ h(par)\ h(title)}$ See Davila (1990)
Content: h(1): Genesis 1:8-10; h(2): 2:17-18; h(par): 12:4-5; h(title): a tab with the word *Genesis*
Bibliography: plates: ER 560 (41.996), 972 (42.723), 1212 (43.157); Davila (1988, 1990, forthcoming)
Date: late Hasmonean to early Herodian
Significance: Four tiny fragments that may not belong to the same manuscript.

Name: 4QGen^j
Content: Portions of Genesis 41–43, 45
Bibliography: plate: ER 1091 (43.007); Davila (1988)
Date: late Hasmonean to early Herodian

Name: 4QGen^k
Content: Genesis 1:9, 14-16, 27-26(transposed); 2:1-3; 3:1-2
Bibliography: plate: ER 1092 (43.008); Davila (1988, 1990, forthcoming)
Date: Herodian formal handwriting (c. A.D. 1–30)
Significance: In Genesis 1:9 this manuscript has the same longer reading as in the Old Greek tradition, which is not included in MT and 4QGen^{b,g}.

Name: 4QpaleoGen(+Exod)^l
Content: Genesis 50:26(?). Although only a few letters of one word survive, these letters, which occur in the last verse of Genesis, are followed by several blank lines and are positioned in the fragment to clearly indicate that this scroll originally contained both the book of Genesis and Exodus. See 4Qpaleo(Gen+)Exod below for the contents of the rest of this manuscript.
Bibliography: McLean (1982); DJD 9, plates I–VI
Date: c. 100 B.C.

Name: 4QpaleoGen^m (formerly 4QpaleoGen^l)
Content: Genesis 26:21-26
Bibliography: DJD 9, plate VI
Date: c. 150 B.C.
Significance: There are only a few orthographic variants from the MT in this small fragment.

Name: 4QExod(+Gen)^a
Content: portions of Exodus 1–8 (or 9)
Bibliography: plates Exodus: ER 665 (42.158), 1090 (43.006) +, 1094 (43.010); Genesis: ER 658 (42.151), 1093 (43.009); Davila (1988, 1991, forthcoming)
Date: c. 125–100 B.C.

Name: 4QExod^b (formerly designated 4QExod^a)
Content: Exodus 1:1-5
Bibliography: plates: ER 664 (42.157, 42.728); ALQ, plate opposite p. 141
Date: uncertain
Significance: This small fragment contains a number of textual variants which, according to Cross, places it in the Egyptian textual tradition, whose primary witness is the LXX. This manuscript may point to an Egyptian text type superior to the Hebrew text used by the Septuagint translators. Cross considers "Egyptian" one of the three recensions of the period, with a geographic orientation.

Name: 4QExod^c
Content: Exodus 15:16-18 + (8 fragments)
Bibliography: plates: ER 666 (42.159), 667 (42.160), 982 (42.734), 1095 (43.011), 1097 (43.013); Cross (1968)
Date: uncertain

Name: 4QExod^d
Content: Exodus 13:15-16

Bibliography: plate ER 1096 (43.012)
Date: uncertain

Name: 4QExod^e
Content: Includes Exodus 13:3-5, 15-16; full contents to be published in DJD 10
Bibliography: plate ER 1096 (43.012)
Date: uncertain

Name: 4QExod^f
Content: Exodus 40:8-27
Bibliography: plate: ER 916 (42.586); ALQ 33, 121; Freedman *Textus* 2 (1962) 93; SWDS 14, 23
Date: mid third century B.C.—"the oldest biblical manuscript in existence (Cross 1965:23)."

Name: 4QExod^g
Content: Includes Exodus 14:21-27; full contents to be published in DJD 10
Bibliography: plates: ER 975 (42.726), 1096 (43.012)
Date: uncertain

Name: 4QExod^h
Content: Includes Exodus 6:4-5; full contents to be published in DJD 10
Bibliography: plate: ER 1096 (43.012)
Date: uncertain

Name: 4QExod^j
Content: to be published in DJD 10
Bibliography: plate: ER 926 (42.603)
Date: uncertain

Name: 4QExod^k
Content: Includes Exodus 26:8-9 (or 2-3); full contents to be published in DJD 10
Bibliography: plate: ER 1096 (43.012)
Date: uncertain

Name: 4Qpaleo(Gen+)Exod^l
Content: Exodus 1:1-5; 2:10, 22-25; 3:1-4, 17-21; 8:13-15, 19-21; 9:25-29, 33-35; 10:1-5; 11:4-10 ; 12:1-11, 42-46; 14:15-24; 16:2-7, 13-14, 18-20, 23-25, 26-31, 33-35; 17:1-3, 5-11; 18:17-24; 19:24-25; 20:1-2; 22:23-24; 23:5-16; 25:7-20; 26:29-37; 27:1, 6-14; 28:33-35, 40-42; 36:34-36. There are an additional 26 fragments which are too small or too poorly preserved to be identified with any certainty.
Bibliography: plates: ER 1013 (42.802), 1084 (42.976), 1014 (42.803); McLean (1982); Sanderson (1990)
Date: uncertain

Name: 4QpaleoExod^m
Content: Exodus 6:25-30; 7:1-19, 29; 8:1[5, EVV], 12-22[16-26, EVV];

9:5-16, 19-21, 35; 10:1-12, 19-28; 11:8-10; 12:1-2, 6-8, 13-15, 17-22, 31-32, 34-39; 13:3-7, 12-13; 14:3-5, 8-9, 25-26; 15:23-27; 16:1, 4-5, 7-8, 31-35; 17:1-16; 18:1-27; 19:1, 7-17, 23-25; 20:1, 18-19; 21:5-6, 13-14, 22-32; 22:3-4, 6-7, 11-13, 16-19, 20-30; 23:15-16, 19-31; 24:1-4, 6-11; 25:11-12, 20-29, 31-34; 26:8-15, 21-30; 27:1-3, 9-14, 18-19; 28:3-4, 8-12, 22-24, 26-28, 30-43; 29:1-5, 20, [v. 21 is omitted] 22-25, 31-41; 30:10 [follows chapter 26]; 30:12-18, 29-31, 34-38 [in MT order]; 31:1-8, 13-15; 32:2-19, 25-30; 33:12-23; 34:1-3, 10-13, 15-18, 20-24, 27-28; 35:1; 36:21-24; 37:9-16

Bibliography: Sanderson (1986); DJD 9, plates VII–XXXIII

Date: c. 200–175 B.C.

Significance: This manuscript has provided important evidence for a new understanding of the early history of the text of the Old Testament. 4QpaleoExod^m shares a number of readings with the Samaritan Pentateuch as well as the Hebrew Vorlage of the LXX. Initially scholars were struck by the many agreements with the Samaritan Pentateuch. It was generally believed that the differences between the Samaritan Pentateuch and the proto-MT were frequently the result of sectarian Samaritan revision. To be sure, there are a few examples of theological "bias," such as in Exodus 20:17, where the tenth commandment imports the statement from Deuteronomy 11:29 regarding the importance of Mt. Gerizim as the center of worship. Most differences, however, reflect nonsectarian differences which are now known to have existed already in the first century B.C. or earlier. According to Sanderson there were four major early witnesses to the text of Exodus: 4Q, the Samaritan Pentateuch, proto-MT, and the LXX. However, there is still no scholarly consensus whether these witnesses should be described as distinct recensions or as evidence of a plurality of text types during this crucial era in the history of the text of the Old Testament. See Sanderson (1986:325-343) for a complete list of variants.

Name: 4QpaleoExod^n is now designated 4QpaleoGen+Exod^l

Name: 4QpapGkExodpar (+4Q127)

Content: It is clear from words such as *Moses, Egypt,* and *Pharaoh* easily identified in the eighty fragments of this manuscript that the text deals with the events of the exodus. However, computer searches have failed to identify specific passages in Exodus. Thus, the manuscript is described as a paraphrase of Exodus. There are several other Qumran manuscripts that are biblical paraphrases.

Bibliography: Ulrich (1990); DJD 9, plate XLVII

Date: c. 150 B.C.–A.D. 50

Significance: This previously unknown work adds to our witnesses another biblical paraphrase—a genre that was popular at the turn of the era. DJD 9 includes other biblical paraphrases.

Name: 4QLev (+Num)^a

Content: Exodus 15:20-23; 16:22-28; 27:10-12; full contents to be published in DJD 10

Bibliography: plates: ER 992 (42.744), 995 (42.747), 1118 (43.034), 1119 (43.035), 1123 (43.039), 1134 (43.050)
Date: uncertain

Name: 4QLev[b]
Content: Leviticus 1:11-17; 2:1-2, 5-8; 22:9-33; 23:2-8, 11-14, 16-22; 24:3-23; 25:28-29, 45-49; full contents to be published in DJD 10
Bibliography: plates: ER 1122 (43.038), 1126 (43.042), 1127 (43.043)
Date: uncertain

Name: 4QLev[c]
Content: Leviticus 4:13-14; full contents to be published in DJD 10
Bibliography: plates: ER 239 (41.298), 1125 (43.041), 1212 (43.157), 1410 (43.437)
Date: uncertain

Name: 4QLev[d]
Content: Leviticus 14:26-30, 33-37; 15:20-24; 17:1-12
Bibliography: plates: ER 989 (42.741), 1124 (43.040); Tov (1992b) (Tov gives PAM no. 43.046, but contents correspond to ER 1124)
Date: uncertain

Name: 4QtgLev
Content: Leviticus 16:12-15, 18-21
Bibliography: DJD 6
Date: c. 100 B.C.

Name: 4QgkLev[a] (= Rahlfs 801)
Content: Leviticus 26:2-16
Bibliography: Skehan (1957); DJD 9, plate XXXVIII
Date: c. 100 B.C.
Significance: Ulrich (1984) lists variants for this and all other Greek Old Testament manuscripts found at Qumran.

Name: 4QpapGkLev[b]
Content: Leviticus 1:11; 2:3-5, 7-8(?); 3:4, 7, 9-14; 4:4, 6-8, 10-11, 18-19, 26-28, 30; 5:6, 8-10, 16-19; 6:1-5 [5:24, MT].
Bibliography: DJD 9, plates XXXIX–XLI.
Date: probably first century B.C.
Significance: See Ulrich (1984) for variants.

Name: 4QNum (+Lev)[a]
Content: Includes Numbers 1:36-40; 2:31-32; 3:5-8, 10-18; 4:2-3, 5-11, 40-44, 47; 5:3-4; 8:7-12; 9:3-10, 19-20; 12:4-11; 13:18; full contents to be published in DJD 10
Bibliography: plates: ER 992 (42.744), 995 (42.747), 1118 (43.034), 1119 (43.035), 1123 (43.039), 1134 (43.050)
Date: uncertain

Name: 4QNum[b]
Content: Numbers 11:31-35; 12:1(?)-6, 8-11; 13:7, 10-13, 15-24; 15:41–

16:11; 17:12-17; 18:25–19:6; 20:12-13b (= Sam. add), 16-17, 19-29(?); 21:1(?)-2, 12a-13a (= Sam. add); 22:5-21, 31-34, 37-38, 41–23:4, 6, 13-15, 21-22, 27–24:10; 25:4-8, 16-18; 26:1-5, 7-10, 12, 14-34, 62–27:5, 7-8, 10, 18-19, 21-23b (= Sam. add); 28:13-17, 28, 30-31; 29:10-13, 16-18, 26-30; 30:1-3, 5-9, 15-16; 31:2-6, 21b-25, 30-33, 35-36, 38, 43-44, 46–32:1, 7-10, 13-17, 19, 23-30, 35, 37-39, 41; 33:1-4, 23, 25, 28, 31, 45, 47-48, 50-52; 34:4-9, 19-21, 23; 35:3-5, 12, 14-15, 18-25, 27-28, 33–36:2, 4-7

Bibliography: plates: ER 197 (41.191), 204 (41.198), 735 (42.244), 998-9 (42.750-1), 1003-4 (42.755-6), 1130 (43.406), 1132-3 (43.048-9) +; Jastram (1990)

Date: c. 30 B.C.–A.D. 20

Significance: There are three clearly distinguishable textual traditions in Numbers: the MT; the Samaritan Pentateuch, which differs primarily from MT in some expansionistic elements and interpolations from Deuteronomy; and the LXX. 4QNum[b] provides evidence for even greater diversity. This text includes the major Samaritan Pentateuch interpolations, but it also shows some agreements with the LXX, and even more significantly, it also contains some unique expansions. The diversity of textual traditions for Numbers is striking.

Name: 4QgkNum (= Rahlfs 803)
Content: Numbers 3:40-42; 4:6-9, 11-14
Bibliography: plates: ER 1327 (PAM 43.291) + ER 603 (PAM 42.039) and ER 518 (PAM 41.933); Skehan (1957:155-156); DJD 9, plates XLII-XLIII
Date: uncertain
Significance: See Ulrich (1984) for variants.

Name: 4QDeut[a]
Content: Deuteronomy 23:26(?); 24:1-8
Bibliography: plates: ER 1154 (43.070), 1186 (43.102); White (1988)
Date: c. 175–150 B.C.
Significance: This manuscript is one of the earliest copies of Deutero-nomy found at Qumran. Although fragmentary, the text appears to be quite close to the presumed original form of the text of Deuteronomy.

Name: 4QDeut[b]
Content: Deuteronomy 29:24-27; 30:3-14; 31:9-17, 24–32:3
Bibliography: plates: ER 1148 (43.064), 1215 (43.160), 1763 (44.083); Duncan (1989)
Date: early Hasmonean (c. 150–100 B.C.)
Significance: This manuscript does not demonstrate a clear textual affilia-tion, but there may be room for the OG longer text of 31:14, 15 in the gap between two fragments.

Name: 4QDeut[c]
Content: Deuteronomy 3:25-26; 4:13-17, 31-32; 7:3-4; 8:1-5; 9:11-12, 17-19, 29; 10:1-2, 5-8; 11:2-4, 9-13, 18-19; 12:18-19, 26, 30-31; 13:5-7, 11-

12, 16; 15:1-5, 15-19; 16:2-3, 5-11, 20–17:7, 15–18:1; 26:19; 27:1-2, 24-26; 28:1-14, 18-20, 22-25, 29-30, 48-50, 61; 29:17-19; 31:16-19; 33:3

Bibliography: plates: ER 954 (42.705), 1149 (43.065), 1151 (43.067), 1153 (43.069), 1721 (44.016); White (1988)

Date: c. 125–100 B.C.

Significance: This manuscript preserves the largest amount of Deuteronomy among the Cave 4 material. Based on line-length studies, it appears that Deuteronomy 32 was written in poetic lines. Its readings generally agree with the LXX.

Name: 4QDeut^d

Content: Deuteronomy 2:26-33; 3:14-29; 4:1

Bibliography: plates: ER 1150 (43.066), 1215 (43.160), 1258 (43.221); White (1988)

Date: c. 100 B.C.

Significance: The orthography of this manuscript is defective—that is, the use of vowel letters is even less than in the proto-MT.

Name: 4QDeut^e

Content: Deuteronomy 3:24; 7:12-16, 21-26(?); 8:1-16

Bibliography: plate: 1152 (43.068); Duncan (1989)

Date: c. 50–25 B.C.

Significance: These small fragments contain no significant variants.

Name: 4QDeut^f

Content: Deuteronomy 4:23-27; 7:21-26; 8:2-14; 9:6-7; 17:17-18; 18:6-10, 18-22; 19:17-21; 20:1-6; 21:4-12; 22:12-19; 23:21-26; 24:2-7; 25:3-9; 26:18–27:10

Bibliography: plates: ER 1146 (43.062), 1149 (43.065); White (1988)

Date: 75–50 B.C.

Name: 4QDeut^g

Content: Deuteronomy 9:12-14; 23:18-20; 24:16-20; 25:1-5, 14-19; 26:2-5; 28:21-24, 27-29

Bibliography: plates: ER 1147 (43.063), 1215 (43.160); White (1988)

Date: c. A.D. 25

Significance: The text and orthography are identical to the MT.

Name: 4QDeut^h

Content: Deuteronomy 1:1-17, 22-23, 29-41, 43–2:5, 28-30; 19:21; 31:9-10; 33:9-11

Bibliography: plate: ER 960 (42.711); Duncan (1989)

Date: c. 50–1 B.C.

Name: 4QDeut^i

Content: Deuteronomy 20:9-13; 21:23; 22:1-9; 23:6-17, 22-26; 24:1

Bibliography: plate: ER 1150 (43.066); White (1988)

Date: c. 75 B.C.

Significance: Contains some significant agreements with OG.

Name: 4QDeut^j
Content: Deuteronomy 5:1-11, 13-15, 21-33; 6:1-3; 8:5-10; 11:6-10, 12-13; 32:7-8—with Exodus 12:43-51; 13:1-5(?).
Bibliography: plates: ER 1135 (43.051), 1137-8 (43.053-4); Duncan (1989)
Date: c. A.D. 50

Name: 4QDeut$^{k1, k2}$ (may be three MSS)
Content: ^{k1}: Deuteronomy 5:28-31; 11:6-13; 32:17-18, 22-23, 25-27; ^{k2}: Deuteronomy 19:8-16; 20:6-19; 23:22-25; 24:1-3; 25:19; 26:1-4, 18-19
Bibliography: plate: ER 1142 (43.056); Duncan (1989); Christensen (1991); Tov (1986:53)
Date: Herodian
Significance: Fragments 1, 2, 9, and 10 (4QDeut^{k1}) are larger writing than fragments 3–8 (4QDeut^{k2}). Otherwise, there are a number of similarities in the handwriting.

Name: 4QDeut^l
Content: Deuteronomy 10:12, 14; 28:67-68; 29:2-5; 31:12; 33:1-2; 34:4-6, 8
Bibliography: plate: ER 1136 (43.052); Duncan (1989)
Date: c. 50 B.C., semi-cursive

Name: 4QDeut^m
Content: Deuteronomy 3:18-21; 4:32-33; 7:19-22
Bibliography: plates: ER 933 (42.632), 963 (42.714); Duncan (1989)
Date: uncertain

Name: 4QDeut^n (All Souls Deuteronomy)
Content: Deuteronomy 5:1-33; 6:1; 8:5-10
Bibliography: plates: ER 941 (42.642), 950-1 (42.701-2); SWDS, plate 19 (called 4QDeut^m); White (1988, 1990a, 1990b); Eshel (1991)
Date: early Herodian (c. 30 B.C.)
Significance: The manuscript has full orthography.

Name: 4QDeut^o
Content: Deuteronomy 4:31-34; 5:1-3, 8-9; 28:15-18, 33-35, 47-49, 51-52, 58-62; 29:22-25
Bibliography: plate: ER 1139 (43.055); Duncan (1989)
Date: uncertain

Name: 4QDeut^p
Content: Deuteronomy 6:4-6, 8-10
Bibliography: plates: ER 1139 (43.055), 1147 (43.063); Duncan (1989)
Date: uncertain

Name: 4QDeut^q
Content: Deuteronomy 32:37-43
Bibliography: plate: ER 932 (42.632); Skehan (1954)
Date: uncertain

Name: 4QpaleoDeut[r]
Content: Deuteronomy 1:8(?); 7:2-7, 16-25; 11:28, 30-32; 12:1-5, 11-12, 22; 13:19; 14:1-4, 19-22, 26-29; 15:5-6, 8-10; 19:2-3; 22:3-7, 12-15; 28:15-18, [omits v. 19], 20; 31:29; 32:6-8, 10-11, 13-14, 33-35; 33:2-8, 29; 34:1. There are 21 other fragments that are too small or poorly preserved to identify.
Bibliography: McLean (1982); DJD 9, plates XXXIV–XXXVI
Date: c. 50 B.C.

Name: 4QpaleoDeut[s]
Content: Deuteronomy 26:14-15
Bibliography: DJD 9, plate XXXVII
Date: c. 250 B.C.
Significance: Agrees with MT in text and orthography.

Name: 4QgkDeut (= Rahlfs 819)
Content: Deuteronomy 11:4 (fragment *a*). Fragments *b* to *f* are too small to identify.
Bibliography: Ulrich (1984); DJD 9, plate XLII
Date: possibly c. 150 B.C.

Name: 4QJosh[a]
Content: Fragments from Joshua 2–10, including 6:5-10; 7:12-15; 8:3-5, 7-9; 10:3-11
Bibliography: plates: ER 1141 (43.057), 1144 (43.060); Tov (1986:321-2); Greenspoon (1992)
Date: uncertain
Significance: "fragmentary in nature, but rather extensive and often different from proto-MT. The ending of chapter 8 . . . differs much from all other known sources (Tov 1986:322)."

Name: 4QJosh[b]
Content: Joshua 2:11-12; 3:15-16; 4:1-3; 17:11-15
Bibliography: plate: ER 1145 (43.061); Boling (1975:110); Greenspoon (1992)
Date: uncertain

Name: 4QJudg[a]
Content: Judges 6:2-6, 11-13
Bibliography: plate: ER 1143 (43.059); Trebolle (1989)
Date: uncertain
Significance: Lacks *wlgmlyhm* (and their camels) of MT, in agreement with Old Latin, in v. 5. The Old Latin has other significant textual variants in this chapter.

Name: 4QJudg[b]
Content: Judges 19:5-7; 21:12-25
Bibliography: plates: ER 1143 (43.059), 1212 (43.157); Trebolle (1991)
Date: Herodian, formal hand

Significance: The text generally agrees with the proto-MT. See 1QJudg for a witness that differs somewhat from the proto-MT.

Name: 4QRuth[a]
Content: to be published in DJD 12
Bibliography: plate: ER 1174 (43.090) +
Date: uncertain

Name: 4QRuth[b]
Content: Ruth 1:1-2, 12-15
Bibliography: plates: ER 1174 (43.090), 1216 (43.161)
Date: uncertain

Name: 4QSam[a]
Content: 1 Samuel 1:2-28; 2:1-6, 8-11, 13-36; 3:1-4, 18-20; 4:9-12; 5:8-12; 6:1-7, 12-13, 16-18, 20-21; 7:1; 8:9-20; 9:6-8, 11-12, 16-24; 10:3-18, 25-27; 11:1, 7-12; 12:7-8, 14-19; 14:24-25, 28-34, 47-51; 15:24-32; 17:3-6; 24:4-5, 8-9, 14-23; 25:3-12, 20-21, 25-26, 39-40; 26:10-12, 21-23; 27:8-12; 28:1-2, 22-25; 30:28-30; 31:2-4; 2 Samuel 2:5-16, 25-27, 29-32; 3:1-8, 23-39; 4:1-4, 9-12; 5:1-16 (omit 4-5); 6:2-9, 12-18; 7:23-29; 8:2-8; 10:4-7, 18-19; 11:2-12, 16-20; 12:4-5, 8-9, 13-20, 30-31; 13:1-6, 13-34, 36-39; 14:1-3, 18-19; 15:1-6, 27-31; 16:1-2, 11-13, 17-18, 21-23; 18:2-7, 9-11; 19:7-12; 20:2-3, 9-14, 23-26; 21:1-2, 4-6, 15-17; 22:30-51; 23:1-6; 24:16-20
Bibliography: plates: ER 1191-3 (43.107-9), 1196-1200 (43.109-117), 1202-3 (43.119-120), 1205-7 (43.122-4) +; Ulrich (1978)
Date: c. 50–25 B.C.
Significance: Although the manuscript preserves only 10 percent of the books of 1 and 2 Samuel, it has made a substantial contribution to our understanding of the history of the textual tradition. There are a large number of agreements with the LXX, although it is not a pure representative of the Egyptian recension (to use Cross's terminology). The MT of Samuel is generally considered to be quite problematic, with numerous omissions. This Qumran manuscript demonstrates the existence of a Hebrew text that is considered to be superior to the MT in many passages. For a different evaluation that favors many MT readings over readings in this manuscript, see Pisano (1984). See McCarter (1980, 1984) for a full discussion of the textual variants.

Name: 4QSam[b]
Content: 1 Samuel 16:1-11; 19:10-17; 20:27-42; 21:1-10; 23:9-17
Bibliography: plates: ER 922 (42.599), 1156 (43.072), 1160 (43.076) +; Cross (1955), McCarter (1980); Andersen and Freedman (1989)
Date: uncertain
Significance: See McCarter (1980) for a full discussion of the textual variants.

Name: 4QSam[c]
Content: 1 Samuel 25:30-32; 2 Samuel 14:7-33; 15:1-15

Bibliography: plates: ER 155 (43.071), 1161 (43.077) +; Ulrich (1979)
Date: uncertain

Name: 4QKgs (Earlier publications list as [a])
Content: 1 Kings 7:31-41; 8:1-9, 16-18
Bibliography: plate: ER 1163 (43.079) +; McKenzie *Bulletin of the International Organization for Septuagint and Cognate Studies* 19(1986):15-34; Trebolle (1992a)
Date: uncertain
Significance: Contains an additional phrase in 8:16, "to be a prince over," not found in the MT but included in the Chronicles parallel passage (2 Chronicles 6:5).

Name: 4QChr
Content: 2 Chronicles 28:27; 29:1-3
Bibliography: plate: ER 1173 (43.089) +; Trebolle (1992b)
Date: uncertain

Name: 4QEzra
Content: Ezra 4:2-6, 9-11; 5:17; 6:1-5
Bibliography: plate: ER 1173 (43.089) +; Ulrich (1992)
Date: c. 50 B.C.
Significance: ". . . demostrates that the Massoretic *textus receptus* . . . has been very faithfully preserved from one of the plural forms of the texts which circulated in the Second Temple period (Ulrich 1992:153)."

Name: 4QJob[a]
Content: portion of Job chapter 36
Bibliography: plate: ER 1180 (43.096) +
Date: uncertain

Name: 4QJob[b]
Content: Includes Job13:4-5; full contents to be published in DJD 12
Bibliography: plates: ER 1178 (43.094) +
Date: uncertain

Name: 4QpaleoJob[c]
Content: 13:18-20, 23-27; 14:13-18
Bibliography: McLean (1982); DJD 9, plate XXXVII
Date: c. 225–150 B.C.
Significance: Very conservative orthography; no internal *matres lectionis* (vowel letters). The MT, in contrast, uses internal vowel letters six times in the few words preserved here (DJD 9:155).

Name: 4QtgJob
Content: Job 3:5-9; 4:16-21; 5:1-4
Bibliography: DJD 6
Date: uncertain

Name: 4QPs[a]
Content: Psalms 5:9-13; 6:1-4; 25:15; 31:24-25; 33:1-12; 35:2, 14-20, 26-

28; 36:1-9; 38:2-12, 16-23; 71:1-14; 47:2; 53:4-7; 54:1-6; 56:4; 62:13(?); 63:2-4; 66:16-20; 67:1-7; 69:1-19
Bibliography: plate: ER 1111 (43.027) +; Skehan (1978)
Date: c. 150 B.C.
Significance: The text is very close to proto-MT, although the sequence of Psalms deviates from the Hebrew canon.

Name: 4QPs^b
Content: Psalms 91:5-8, 12-15; 92:4-8, 13-15; 93:5; 94:1-4, 8-14, 17-18, 21-22; 96:2; 98:4; 99:5-6; 100:1-2; 102:5(?), 10-29; 103:1-6, 9-14, 20-21; 112:4-5; 113:1; 115:2-3; 116:17-19; 118:1-3, 6-11, 18-20, 23-26, 29
Bibliography: plates: ER 589-90 (42.025-6), 1116 (43.032) +; Skehan (1964)
Date: Herodian
Significance: The orthography is close to the proto-MT.

Name: 4QPs^c
Content: Psalms 16:7-9; 18:3-14, 16-18, 33-41; 27:12-14; 28:1-2, 4; 35:27-28; 37:18-19; 45:8-11; 49:1-17; 50:14-23; 51:1-5; 52:6-11; 53:1
Bibliography: plate: ER 1107 (43.023), 1211 (43.156) +; Skehan (1978)
Date: c. A.D. 50–68
Significance: The orthography is very close to the proto-MT.

Name: 4QPs^d
Content: Psalms 146:10(?); 147:1-3, 13-17, 20; 104:1-5, 8-11, 14-15, 22-25, 33-35
Bibliography: plate: ER 1105 (43.021) +; Skehan (1978)
Date: c. 50 B.C.
Significance: The orthography is close to the proto-MT.

Name: 4QPs^e
Content: Psalms 76:10-12; 77:1; 78:6-7, 31-33; 81:2-3; 86:10-11; 88:1-4; 89:44-46, 50-53; 104:1-3, 20-21; 105:22-24, 36-45; 109:13; 115:15-18; 116:1-3; 120:6; 125:2-5; 126:1-5; 129:8; 130:1-3
Bibliography: plate: ER 1112 (43.028) +; Skehan (1978)
Date: c. A.D. 50
Significance: The manuscript has expanded orthography.

Name: 4QPs^f
Content: Psalms 22:14-17; 107:2-4, 8-11, 13-15, 18-19, 22-30, 35ff.; 109:4-6, 25-28; Apostrophe to Zion; Apostrophe to Judah; Eschatological Hymn
Bibliography: plates: ER 1110 (43.026), 1550 (43.603) +; Skehan (1978)
Date: late Hasmonean
Significance: The manuscript has expanded orthography with inconsistent use of *waw* as a vowel letter.

Name: 4QPs^g
Content: Psalm 119:37-43, 44-46, 49-50, 73, 81-83, 90ff.
Bibliography: plate: ER 1110 (43.026) +; Skehan (1978)
Date: c. A.D. 50

Significance: The manuscript has expanded orthography with extensive use of *waw* as a vowel letter.

Name: 4QPs[h]
Content: Psalm 119:10-21
Bibliography: plate: ER 1110 (43.026) +; Skehan (1978)
Date: c. A.D. 50
Significance: The manuscript has expanded orthography with extensive use of *waw* as a vowel letter.

Name: 4QPs[j]
Content: Psalms 48:1-7; 49:6, 9-12, 15(?), 17(?)
Bibliography: plate: ER 1114 (43.030) +; Skehan (1978)
Date: c. A.D. 50
Significance: The manuscript has expanded orthography with extensive use of *waw* as a vowel letter.

Name: 4QPs[k]
Content: Psalms 26:7-12; 27:1; 30:9-13; 135:7-16;
Skehan classifies fragments from chapters 26, 27, and 30 as 4QPs[r]

Bibliography: plate: ER 1114 (43.030) +; Skehan (1978)
Date: 100–50 B.C.
Significance: The manuscript has sparse orthography.

Name: 4QPs[l]
Content: Psalm 104:3-5, 11-12
Bibliography: plate: ER 1114 (43.030) +; Skehan (1978)
Date: c. 50–1 B.C.
Significance: The manuscript has sparse orthography; it uses *shin* (the penultimate letter of the Hebrew alphabet) for *samek* (the fifteenth letter of the Hebrew alphabet).

Name: 4QPs[m]
Content: Psalms 93:3-5; 95:3-6; 97:6-9; 98:4-8
Bibliography: plate: ER 1114 (43.030) +; Skehan (1978)
Date: probably Herodian
Significance: The manuscript is too fragmentary to characterize.

Name: 4QPs[n]
Content: Psalms 135:6-8, 11-12; 136:23
Bibliography: plate: ER 1114 (43.030) +; Skehan (1978)
Date: c. 25 B.C.

Name: 4QPs[o]
Content: Psalms 114:7-8; 115:1-4; 116:5-10
Bibliography: plate: ER 1114 (43.030) +; Skehan (1978)
Date: probably Herodian
Significance: The manuscript is too fragmentary to characterize.

Name: 4QPs[p]
Content: Psalm 143:6-8

Bibliography: plate: ER 1114 (43.030) +; Skehan (1978)
Date: probably Herodian
Significance: The manuscript is too fragmentary to characterize.

Name: 4QPs^q
Content: Psalms 31:25 [Ps. 32 lacking]; 33:1-18; 35:4-20
Bibliography: Skehan (1978)
Date: c. A.D. 50
Significance: The manuscript has full orthography for use of *waw*.

Name: 4QPs^r
Content: Psalms 26:7-12; 27:1; 30:9-13
Bibliography: plate: ER 1114 (43.030) +; Skehan (1978)
Date: probably Herodian
Significance: The manuscript is too fragmentary to characterize.

Name: 4QPs^s
Content: Psalms 5:8-13; 6:1
Bibliography: plates: ER 1112-3 (43.028-29), 1211 (43.156), 968
  (42.719); Skehan (1981)
Date: c. A.D. 50
Significance: The manuscript has expanded Qumran orthography.

Name: 4QPs frg1
Content: Psalm 42:5
Bibliography: plate: ER 641 (42.081); Skehan (1978)
Date: c. A.D. 50

Name: 4QPs frg2: Sanders (1967)
Content: Psalm 88:12
Bibliography: plate: ER 1105 (43.021)
Date: uncertain

Name: 4QPs frg3: Sanders (1967); frg2: Skehan (1978)
Content: Psalm 99:1
Date: late first century B.C.

Name: 4QPs89
Content: Psalm 89:20-22, 26-28, 31
Bibliography: Milik (1966), Skehan (1978)
Date: uncertain

Name: 4QProv^a
Content: Proverbs 1:27-33; 2:1; parts of chapters 14 and 15(?)
Bibliography: plates: ER 1100 (43.016), 1511 (43.563); Skehan
  (1959)
Date: uncertain

Name: 4QProv^b
Content: Includes Proverbs 14:31-35; 15:1-5, 7-8, 20-31; full contents to
  be published in DJD 12

Bibliography: plates: ER 1100 (43.016), 1511 (43.563)
Date: uncertain

Name: 4QQoh[a]
Content: 5:13-17; 6:(1?), 3-8, 12; 7:1-10, 19-20
Bibliography: plate: ER 1176 (43.092); Muilenberg (1954a); Ulrich (1992b), with plate
Date: c. 175–125 B.C.
Significance: ". . . minor but occasional variants from what later became the traditional text [MT] (Ulrich 1992b:153)."

Name: 4QQoh[b]
Content: 1:10-14 (15?)
Bibliography: plate: ER 1174 (43.090); Ulrich (1992b), with plate
Date: c. 50 B.C.–25 A.D.
Significance: See 4QQoh[a].

Name: 4QCant[a]
Content: Includes 3:7-11; 4:1-7; full contents to be published in DJD 12
Bibliography: plate: ER 1181 (43.097)
Date: uncertain

Name: 4QCant[b]
Content: Includes 2:9-17; 3:1-2; 4:1-11, 14–5:1; full contents to be published in DJD 12
Bibliography: plate: ER 1177 (43.093)
Date: uncertain

Name: 4QCant[c]
Content: Includes 3:7-8; full contents to be published in DJD 12
Bibliography: plate: ER 1181 (43.097)
Date: uncertain

Name: 4QIsa[a]
Content: Isaiah 1:1-3; 2:7-10; 4:5-6; 6:4-7; 11:12-15; 12:4-6; 13:4-6; 17:9-14; 19:9-14; 20:1-6; 21:1-2, 4-16; 22:13-25; 23:1-12
Bibliography: plate: ER 1099 (43.015) +; Skehan (1979); Muilenberg (1954b) for chapters 22 and 23
Date: c. 25 B.C.
Significance: Many of the Isaiah manuscripts from Cave 4 are quite fragmentary. They are fully collated in F. J. Morrow's dissertation (1973), where all Isaiah manuscripts known to him are treated in a single chapter-by-chapter survey. Morrow also categorizes the textual variants (pages 191-204) and finds, in addition to orthographic variants, numerous examples of "modernizations" in both vocabulary and grammar. However, the text of Isaiah does not display clearly differentiated recensions or text types such as we have in Exodus, 1 and 2 Samuel, and Jeremiah.

Name: 4QIsa[b]
Content: Isaiah 1:1-6; 2:3-16; 3:14-22; 5:15-28; 9:10-11; 11:7-9; 12:2;

69

13:3-18; 17:8-14; 18:1, 5-7; 19:1-25; 20:1-4; 21:11-14; 22:24-25; 24:2;
26:1-5, 7-19; 35:9-10; 36:1-2; 37:29-32; 39:1-8; 40:1-4, 22-26; 41:8-11;
43:12-15; 44:19-28; 45:20-25; 46:1-3; 49:21-23; 51:14-16; 52:2, 7;
53:11-12; 61:1-3; 64:5-11; 65:1; 66:24
Bibliography: plates: ER 1101 (43.017), 1115 (43.031) +; Skehan (1979)
Date: c. 25 B.C., poorly written
Significance: See 4QIsaᵃ.

Name: 4QIsaᶜ
Content: Isaiah 9:3-12; 10:23-32; 11:4-11, 15-16; 12:1; 14:1-5; 21:25;
22:10-14; 23:8-18; 24:1-15, 19-23; 25:1-2, 8-12; 30:8-17; 33:2-8, 16-
23; 45:1-4, 6-13; 48:10-13, 17-19; 50:7-11; 51:1-16; 52:10-15; 53:1-3,
6-8; 54:3-17; 55:1-6; 66:20-24
Bibliography: plates: ER 1104 (43.020), 1106 (43.022), 1113 (43.029) +;
Skehan (1979)
Date: c. A.D. 50–68
Significance: See 4QIsaᵃ.

Name: 4QIsaᵈ
Content: Isaiah 46:10-13; 47:1-6, 8-9; 48:8-22; 49:1-15; 52:4-7; 53:8-12;
54:1-11; 57:9-21; 58:1-3, 5-7
Bibliography: plates: ER 1102-3 (43.018-9) +; Skehan (1979)
Date: early Herodian
Significance: See 4QIsaᵃ.

Name: 4QIsaᵉ
Content: Isaiah 8:2-14; 9:17-20; 10:1-10
Bibliography: plate: ER 1109 (43.025) +; Skehan (1979)
Date: c. 25–1 B.C.
Significance: See 4QIsaᵃ.

Name: 4QIsaᶠ
Content: Isaiah 1:10-16, 18-31; 2:1-3; 5:13-14, 25; 6:3-8, 10-13; 7:16-18,
23-25; 8:1, 4-11; 20:4-6; 22:15-22, 25; 24:1-3; 28:6-9, 16-18, 22, 28-29;
29:1-7, 8(?)
Bibliography: plate: ER 1108 (43.024) +; Skehan (1979)
Date: late Hasmonean
Significance: See 4QIsaᵃ.

Name: 4QIsaᵍ
Content: Isaiah 42:14-25; 43:1-4, 17-24
Bibliography: plates: ER 1098 (43.014), 1217 (43.162) +; Skehan (1979)
Date: c. 25–1 B.C.
Significance: See 4QIsaᵃ.

Name: 4QIsaʰ
Content: Isaiah 7:14-15; 8:11-14; 42:2, 4-11; 56:7-8; 57:5-8; 59:15-16;
60:20-22; 61:1-2
Bibliography: plates: ER 1098 (43.014), 1109 (43.025) +; Skehan
(1979)

Date: second century B.C.
Significance: See 4QIsa^a.

Name: 4QIsa^j
Content: Isaiah 1:1-6
Bibliography: plate: ER 1113 (43.029) +; Skehan (1979)
Date: c. 50–25 B.C.
Significance: See 4QIsa^a.

Name: 4QIsa^k
Content: Isaiah 28:26-29; 29:1-9
Bibliography: plate: ER 1103 (43.019) +; Skehan (1979)
Date: late Hasmonean
Significance: See 4QIsa^a.

Name: 4QIsa^l
Content: Isaiah 2:1-4; 7:17-20; 11:14-15; 12:1-4, 6; 13:1-4; 14:1-12, 21-24
Bibliography: plates: ER 1109 (43.025), 1327 (43.291) +; Skehan (1979)
Date: early Herodian
Significance: See 4QIsa^a.

Name: 4QIsa^m
Content: Isaiah 61:3-6
Bibliography: plate: ER 1098 (43.014) +; Skehan (1979)
Date: late Hasmonean
Significance: See 4QIsa^a.

Name: 4QIsa^n
Content: Isaiah 58:13-14
Bibliography: plate: ER 1098 (43.014) +; Skehan (1979)
Date: late Hasmonean
Significance: See 4QIsa^a.

Name: 4QIsa^o
Content: Isaiah 14:28-32; 15:1; 16:7-8(?)
Bibliography: plate: ER 1098 (43.014) +; Skehan (1979)
Date: Herodian
Significance: The manuscript displays the final form of the *mem* (the thir-teenth letter of the Hebrew alphabet) in the middle of words.

Name: 4QIsa^p
Content: Isaiah 5:28-30
Bibliography: plate: ER 1098 (43.014) +; Skehan (1979)
Date: first century B.C.
Significance: See 4QIsa^a.

Name: 4QIsa^q
Content: Isaiah 54:11-13
Bibliography: plate: ER 1102 (43.018) +; Skehan (1979)
Date: Herodian
Significance: See 4QIsa^a.

Name: 4QIsa^r

Content: uncertain; not listed in Skehan (1979) or in Reed's inventory (1991-2)

Name: 4QJer^a

Content: Jeremiah 7:29-34; 8:1(?)-6; 9:1(?)-2, 7-14; 10:9-14; 11:3-6; 12:3-6, 13-17; 13:1-7; 14:4-7; 15:1-2; 17:8-26; 18:15-23; 19:1; 22:4-16

Bibliography: plates: ER 1159 (43.075), ER 1253 (43.216) +; Janzen (1973), not all columns reported. Tov (1989) reports fifteen columns between 7:1 and 26:10

Date: c. 200 B.C. (Cross); late third or early second century B.C. (Yardeni)

Significance: The manuscript generally follows proto-MT. As noted above in the entry for 2QJer, there are significant differences between the MT and LXX texts of Jeremiah. The LXX is shorter by at least one-eighth, and a number of chapters are arranged in a different sequence. One of the striking aspects of the Jeremiah manuscripts found in Cave 4 is the existence of copies of the book that follow proto-MT (including 4QJer^a and 4QJer^c) and 4QJer^b, which resembles the LXX. This evidence clearly demonstrates that both editions of Jeremiah were in existence before the Christian era and that a single community possessed both editions.

Name: 4QJer^b

Content: Jeremiah 9:22-26; 10:1-18

Bibliography: plates: ER 154 (41.146), 759 (42.280), 1162 (43.078) +; Tov (1989, 1992d). Yardeni (1990) discusses in detail the orthography of this manuscript.

Date: Hasmonean (Cross)

Significance: The text resembles LXX arrangement and shortness; the orthography is proto-MT.

Name: 4QJer^c

Content: Jeremiah 4:5, 13-16; 8:1-3, 21-23; 9:1-5; 10:12-13; 19:8-9(?); 20:1-5(?), 7-9(?), [12]-15; 21:7-10; 22:4-6, 10-28; 25:7-8, 15-17, 24-26; 26:10-13; 27:1-3, 13-15; 30:[4]-24; 31:1-14, [15]-26; 33:16-20

Bibliography: plates: ER 1185 (43.101), ER 1187-90 (43.103-6) +; Tov (1991)

Date: uncertain

Significance: The text is very close to proto-MT. Most of the differences are insignificant. See Tov (1990:272-273) for a full collation and categorization of the textual variants.

Name: 4QJer^d (earlier reported as part of 4QJer^b)

Content: Jeremiah 43:2-10

Bibliography: plates: ER 65 (40.602), 154 (41.146), 759 (42.280), 1162 (43.078); Tov (1989, 1992d)

Date: uncertain

Name: 4QJer^e (earlier reported as part of 4QJer^b)

Content: Jeremiah 50:4-6

Bibliography: plates: ER 220 (41.278), 565 (42.001), 759 (42.280), 1162 (43.078); Tov (1989)
Date: uncertain

Name: 4QLam (sometimes reported as 4QLam[a])
Content: Lamentations 1:1-16
Bibliography: plates: ER 1179 (43.095), 1216 (43.161); Cross (1983)
Date: uncertain

Name: 4QEzek[a]
Content: Ezekiel 10:5-15, 17-22; 11:1-10; 23:14-18, 44-47; 41:3-6
Bibliography: plate: ER 1166 (43.088) +; Lust (1986)
Date: Herodian
Significance: The text generally agrees with the MT.

Name: 4QEzek[b]
Content: Ezekiel 1:10-13, 16-17, 20-24
Bibliography: plate: ER 1172 (43.088) +; Lust (1986)
Date: early Herodian
Significance: The text generally agrees with the MT.

Name: 4QEzek[c]
Content: Includes Ezekiel 24:2-3; full contents to be published in DJD 12
Bibliography: plate: ER 1172 (43.088)
Date: uncertain

Name: 4QDan[a]
Content: Daniel 1:16-20; 2:9-11, 19-49; 3:1-2; 4:29-30; 5:5-7, 12-14, 16-19; 7:5-7, 25-28; 8:1-5; 10:16-20; 11:13-16
Bibliography: Ulrich (1987) with plates
Date: late Hasmonean or early Herodian
Significance: In Daniel 1:20 there appears to be a gap in the extant fragments that would be about the size necessary to include the longer text found in the Greek manuscript 967. The Greek Daniel exists in two distinctively different versions. The "Theodotionic" version supplanted the Old Greek version in the LXX, but the other version is found in a few manuscripts, including 967 (Chester Beatty Papyrus IX).

Name: 4QDan[b]
Content: Daniel 5:10-12, 14-16, 19-22; 6:8-22, 27-29; 7:1-6, 11(?), 26-28; 8:1-8, 13-16
Bibliography: Ulrich (1989) with plates
Date: c. A.D. 20–50

Name: 4QDan[c]
Content: Daniel 10:5-9, 11-16, 21; 11:1-2, 13-17, 25-29
Bibliography: Ulrich (1989) with plates
Date: c. 125–100 B.C.. This would date this manuscript only about fifty years younger than the date of the autograph of the book of Daniel

73

given by many scholars, i.e., about 168–165 B.C., the time of the Macca-
bean revolt.

Name: 4QDan^d
Content: only a few small scraps (Ulrich 1990:30)
Bibliography: plates: ER 1128 (43.044), 1168 (43.084)
Date: uncertain

Name: 4QDan^e
Content: only a few small scraps (Ulrich 1990:30)
Bibliography: plate: ER 1178 (43.094)
Date: uncertain

Name: 4QXII^a
Content: Zechariah 14:18; Malachi 2:10–3:24 (=4:6 EVV); Jonah 1:1-2,
   8-9, 16; 2:7; 3:2 (may have followed Malachi)
Bibliography: plates: ER 1182-4 (43.098-100), 1257 (43.220) +; Fuller
   (1988, 1991)
Date: early Hasmonean, semi-cursive; c. 100–50 B.C.
Significance: The MS has two unique readings: 2:14 may be superior to
   proto-MT; 2:16b probably inferior. It occupies an intermediate position
   between proto-MT and LXX (Fuller 1991).

Name: 4QXII^b
Content: Zephaniah 1:1-2; 2:13-15; 3:19-20; Haggai 1:1-2; 2:2-4
Bibliography: plate: ER 1171 (43.087) +; Fuller (1988)
Date: 150–125 B.C.; early Hasmonean hand

Name: 4QXII^c
Content: Hosea 2:13-15; 3:2-4; 4:1–5:1; 13:4-8, 15; 14:1-6; Joel 1:11-20;
   2:1, 8-23; 4:6-21; Amos 2:11-16; 3:1-15; 4:1-2; 6:13-14; 7:1-16; Zepha-
   niah 2:15; 3:1-2; Malachi 3:6(?)-7
Bibliography: plates: ER 1195 (43.112), 1201 (43.118) +; Fuller (1988)
Date: c. 75 B.C.
Significance: There is "a clear affiliation with [O]G, but there is no clear
   indication that the base texts of M[T] and [O]G differed radically
   (Fuller 1988:104)." The manuscript has *plene* (full) orthography.

Name: 4QXII^d
Content: Hosea 1:7-9; 2:1-5
Bibliography: plate: ER 1175 (43.091) +; Sinclair (1980)
Date: Hasmonean. Of the Qumran biblical manuscripts this script is per-
   haps the most difficult to date (Fuller 1988:106).
Significance: The text agrees with the MT.

Name: 4QXII^e
Content: Haggai 2:20-21; Zechariah 1:4-6, 9-10, 13-14; 2:10-14; 3:4-10;
   4:1-4; 5:8–6:5; 8:3-4, 6-7; 12:7-12
Bibliography: plates: ER 1194 (43.110), 1257 (43.220) +; Fuller (1988)
Date: c. 75 B.C.; late Hasmonean

Significance: Closely related to OG, sharing a number of inferior readings (Fuller 1988:140).

Name: 4QXII^f
Content: Micah 5:1-2; Jonah 1:6-8, 10-16
Bibliography: plate: ER 1175 (43.091) +; Fuller (1988)
Date: c. 50 B.C.; late Hasmonean; formal hand
Significance: The text of Jonah is quite uniform in the ancient witnesses, including 4QXII^f. This manuscript does contain one unique reading in Micah 5:1(2): *l'* for MT *ly*.

Name: 4QXII^g
Content: contains parts of Hosea, Joel, Amos, Zephaniah, and Jonah; largest and perhaps most poorly preserved Minor Prophets scroll from cave 4 (Fuller 1988)
Bibliography: plates: ER 537-8 (41.966-7), 543 (41.976), 546 (41.980), 562 (41.998), 1083 (42.975) +; Fuller (1988)
Date: probably late Hasmonean

Name: 4QXII$^?$
Content: Hosea 13:15b–14:1, 3-6 (according to Testuz)
Bibliography: Testuz (1955)
Date: uncertain

QUMRAN CAVE 5

Name: 5QDeut (= 5Q1)
Content: Deuteronomy 7:15-24; 8:5-20; 9:1-2
Bibliography: DJD 3
Date: first part of second century B.C.
Significance: There are some textual similarities with the Samaritan Pentateuch; the section divisions differ from the MT.

Name: 5QKgs (= 5Q2)
Content: 1 Kings 1:1, 16-17, 27-37
Bibliography: DJD 3
Date: Hasmonean
Significance: This manuscript has the same text as the MT, which is the same as the LXX in 1 Kings 1. Thus, there are no significant variants.

Name: 5QPs (= 5Q5)
Content: Psalm 119:99-101, 104, 113-120, 138-142
Bibliography: DJD 3
Date: first century A.D.
Significance: The first letters in the right margin of two columns show that the manuscript of this Psalm preserved the acrostic arrangement. The *samek* (the fifteenth letter of the Hebrew alphabet) and *tsade* (the eighteenth letter of the Hebrew alphabet) sections are preserved in the fragments.

Name: 5QIsa (= 5Q3)
Content: Isaiah 40:16, 18-19

Bibliography: DJD 3
Date: uncertain
Significance: The fragment is too small to characterize.

Name: 5QLam^a (= 5Q6)
Content: Lamentations 4:5-8, 11-15, 19-22; 5:1-12
Bibliography: DJD 3
Date: first century B.C.
Significance: This manuscript has the same text as the MT, which is the same as the LXX in Lamentations 4. Thus, there are no significant variants.

Name: 5QLam^b (= 5Q7)
Content: Lamentations 4:17-19
Bibliography: DJD 3
Date: first century B.C.
Significance: Quite fragmentary; the MS preserves the *kethib* reading (i.e., the reading in the text as opposed to the reading in the margin of the MT) in Lamentations 4:17.

Name: 5QXII (= 5Q4)
Content: Amos 1:3-5
Bibliography: DJD 3
Date: first century A.D.
Significance: Preserves one word supported by LXX, against the MT, in Amos 1:3 (*hrwt*—meaning "those who are pregnant").

QUMRAN CAVE 6

Name: 6QpaleoGen (= 6Q1)
Content: Genesis 6:13-21
Bibliography: DJD 3
Date: uncertain
Significance: The text and orthography correspond closely with the MT.

Name: 6QpaleoLev (= 6Q2)
Content: Leviticus 8:12-13
Bibliography: DJD 3
Date: uncertain
Significance: Difficult to determine because the fragment is poorly preserved. It has a few vowel letters not found in the MT, but there are no textual variants.

Name: 6QpapDeut(?) (= 6Q3)
Content: Deuteronomy 26:19(?)
Bibliography: DJD 3
Date: uncertain
Significance: The manuscript preserves only one word and parts of two additional letters.

Name: 6QpapKgs (= 6Q4)
Content: 1 Kings 3:12-14; 12:28-31; 22:28-31; 2 Kings 5:26; 6:32; 7:8-10, 20; 8:1-5; 9:1-2; 10:19-21
Bibliography: DJD 3
Date: 150–100 B.C.
Significance: There are some readings with support from the LXX.

Name: 6QpapPs (= 6Q5)
Content: Psalm 78:36-37(?)
Bibliography: DJD 3
Date: uncertain
Significance: Parts of only three words are preserved; identification is uncertain.

Name: 6QCant (= 6Q6)
Content: Song of Solomon 1:1-7
Bibliography: DJD 3
Date: c. A.D. 50
Significance: There are occasional agreements with Vulgate and Syriac.

Name: 6QpapDan (= 6Q7)
Content: Daniel 8:16, 17(?), 20, 21(?); 10:8-16; 11:33-36, 38
Bibliography: DJD 3
Date: c. A.D. 50
Significance: Though very poorly preserved, it generally agrees with the proto-MT.

QUMRAN CAVE 7

Name: 7QpapGkExod (= 7Q1)
Content: Exodus 28:4-7
Bibliography: DJD 3
Date: c. 100 B.C.
Significance: The text is generally close to the proto-MT.

Name: 7Q5
Content: Zechariah 7:4-5 according to Spottorno; Mark 6:52-53(?) and other NT fragments according to O'Callaghan
Bibliography: O'Callaghan (1972); Spottorno (1992)
Date: perhaps c. A.D. 50
Significance: José O'Callaghan began a controversy when he identified the Qumran papyrus fragment as part of the Gospel of Mark (6:52-53). If this identification is accepted, another very small fragment, containing only a few letters, could be located in Mark 4:28. O'Callaghan also proposed an identification of 7Q8 as a fragment of James 1:23-24, based on his reading of this very small fragment. His identifications have received very little support. O'Callaghan's views have recently been revived by Carsten P. Thiede in his book *The Earliest Gospel Manuscript?* (1992). By offering different readings of several letters

which are poorly preserved, Spottorno (1992) locates this fragment in Zechariah 7:4-5 with a textual reading from the Lucianic recension.

QUMRAN CAVE 8

Name: 8QGen (= 8Q1)
Content: Genesis 17:12-19; 18:20-25
Bibliography: DJD 3
Date: Herodian
Significance: There is an interlinear insert at Genesis 18:25 that reads the same as the LXX.

Name: 8QPs (= 8Q2)
Content: Psalms 17:5-9, 14; 18:6-9, 10-13
Bibliography: DJD 3
Date: first century A.D.
Significance: The text and orthography correspond to the proto-MT.

QUMRAN CAVE 11

Name: 11QLev
Content: Leviticus 9:23–10:2
Bibliography: van der Ploeg (1968)
Date: uncertain

Name: 11QpaleoLev
Content: Leviticus 4:24-26; 10:4-7; 11:27-32; 13:3-9, 39-43; 14:16-21, 52-57; 15:2-5; 16:2-4, 34; 17:1-5; 18:27-30; 19:1-4; 20:1-6; 21:6-11; 22:21-27; 23:22-29; 24:9-14; 25:28-36; 26:17-26; 27:11-19
Bibliography: Freedman (1985); Puech (1989)
Date: inconsistency in script, but similar to 4QpaleoExod^m—c. 200 B.C. (Freedman 1985:15)
Significance: "Fifteen unique readings that are inferior to MT (Hartley 1992: xxix).

Name: 11QtgJob
Content: Job 17:14-16; 18:1-4; 19:11-19, 29(?); 20:1-6; 21:1-10, 20-28; 22:2-9, 16-22; 24:12-17, 25; 25:1-6; 26:1-2, 10-14; 27:1-4, 11-20; 28:4-9, 13, 21-28; 29:7-16, 24-25; 30:1-4, 13-20, 27-31; 31:1, 8-16, 26-32, 40; 32:1-3, 11-17; 33:6-16, 24-32; 34:6-17, 24-34; 35:6-15; 36:7-16, 23-33; 37:10-19; 38:3-13, 23-34; 39:1-11, 20-29; 40:5-14, 15(?), 23-31; 41:7-17, 26; 42:1-2 (+40:5), 4-6, 9-11
Bibliography: van der Ploeg (1971); Sokoloff (1974)
Date: Herodian

Name: 11QPs^a
Content: (the numbering of the Psalms reflects the sequence in the MS) Psalms 1:1-8; 102:1-2, 18-29; 103:1; 109:21-31; 118:25-29; 104:1-6, 21-35; 147:1-2, 18-20; 105:1-12, 25-45; 146:1-12, 25-45; 148:1-12; 121:1-8; 122:1-9; 123:1-2; 124:7-8; 125:1-5; 126:1-6; 127:1; 128:4-6; 129:1-8; 130:1-8; 131:1; 132:8-18; 119:1-6, 15-25, 37-49, 59-73, 82-96,

105-112; 135:1-9, 17-21; 136:1-16, 26; 118:1, 15, 16, 8, 9, 29(transposed); 145:1-7, 13-21; 139:8-24; 137:1, 9; 138:1-8; 154:3-19; Plea for
Deliverance; Sirach 51:13-30; 93:1-3; 141:5-10; 133:1-3; 144:1-7, 15;
155:1-19; 142:4-8; 143:1-8; 149:7-9; 150:1-6; Hymn to the Creator;
2 Samuel 23:7; David's Compositions; Psalms 140:1-5; 134:1-3; 151
(or 151A); 152 (or 151B)

Bibliography: DJD 4; Sanders (1967). Sanders edited both the DJD 4 volume and the 1967 edition. The latter publication includes "Fragment E,"
which Yadin had purchased for Israel. He recognized it as a part of
11QPs^a when the bulk of the scroll was published in DJD 4. Fragment E
includes portions of Psalms 118, 104, 147, and 105.

Date: c. A.D. 25–50

Significance: This scroll preserves large portions of twenty-eight columns
and other large fragments. The tetragrammaton is written in paleo-
Hebrew characters. One of the most striking features is the fact that the
Psalms are not arranged in the same sequence as the Hebrew Bible. Further, several other Psalms, some which were known from the ancient
versions and others hitherto unknown in modern times, are intermingled
with the canonical Psalms. Sanders concluded that the arrangement of
the Psalms in 11QPs^a demonstrates that the third part of the Hebrew
canon, in which the book of Psalms is found, was still fluid and not yet
closed in the first century A.D. 11QPs^b, 4QPs^f, and 4QPs^e also follow a
different sequence of Psalms. While many scholars agree with Sanders,
Skehan (1978) believes 11QPs^a is "a liturgical complex" and points to
the fact that the Psalms appear to be arranged in thematic groupings.

Name: 11QPs^b
Content: (the numbering of the Psalms reflects the sequence in the MS)
Psalms 141:10; 133:1-3; Plea for Deliverance; 144:1-2; 118:1(?), 15-16
Bibliography: van der Ploeg (1985-87)
Date: uncertain

Name: 11QPs^c
Content: Psalms 2:1-6; 9:3-7; 12:5-8; 13:2-6; 14:1-6; 17:9-15; 18:1-12;
43:1-3; 77:18-21; 78:1
Bibliography: van der Ploeg (1985-87)
Date: uncertain

Name: 11QPs^c (Sanders's additions—see above)
Content: Psalms 35:15-28; 36:1-13; 37:1-40; 38:1-23; 39:1-14
Bibliography: Sanders (1967:145) assigns fragments from 11QPs^{b,c,d} dif-
ferently than van der Ploeg. In addition, Sanders reports additional frag-
ments from his 11QPs^c, as listed here.
Date: uncertain

Name: 11QPs^d
Content: Psalms 39:13–40:1; 59:5-8; 68:1-5, 16-18; 78:5-12; 81:4-10
Bibliography: van der Ploeg (1985-87)
Date: uncertain

Name: 11QPs^e
Content: Psalm 37:1-4
Bibliography: van der Ploeg (1985-87)
Date: uncertain

Name: 11QPsAp^a
Content: Psalm 91:1-16 (preceded by apocryphal Psalms)
Bibliography: van der Ploeg (1965)
Date: uncertain

Name: 11QEzek
Content: Ezekiel 4:3-5, 9-10; 5:11-17; 7:9-12; 10:11
Bibliography: Brownlee (1963)
Date: c. 55–25 B.C.

MASADA

Name: Mas Gen (or MasJub)
Content: Genesis 46:7-11. Talmon thinks this fragment is actually from the Book of Jubilees, a biblical paraphrase.
Bibliography: Yadin (1965, 1977); Talmon (1989)
Date: This and the other biblical manuscripts found at Masada were found in a location associated with the Jewish revolt of A.D. 66–73, establishing the latest possible date for the copying of the manuscripts. The Genesis fragment is dated to the first century B.C. by Yadin.
Significance: According to Yadin, it contains several slight textual variations from the MT.

Name: Mas Lev^a
Content: Leviticus 4:3-9
Bibliography: Yadin (1965)
Date: uncertain, but before A.D. 73
Significance: The text corresponds throughout to the MT.

Name: Mas Lev^b
Content: portions of Leviticus 8–12
Bibliography: Yadin (1965)
Date: uncertain, but before A.D. 73
Significance: The text is identical to the MT, with spaces between the chapters.

Name: Mas Deut
Content: Deuteronomy 33:17-27; 34:2-6
Bibliography: Yadin (1977)
Date: uncertain, but before A.D. 73
Significance: According to Yadin, the text is virtually identical with the traditional biblical texts.

Name: Mas Ps^a (M1039-1160)
Content: Psalms 81:3-17; 82:1-8; 83:1-19; 84:1-13; 85:1-10 (Sanders and Nebe: 1-6)

Bibliography: Yadin (1965)
Date: late Herodian
Significance: The text is the same as MT, except Psalm 83:6, which reads *'lhy* (gods) for *'hly* (tents).

Name: Mas Ps[b]
Content: Psalm 150:1-6
Bibliography: Yadin (1977)
Date: uncertain, but before A.D. 73
Significance: The text is identical to the MT.

Name: Mas Ezek
Content: fragments of Ezekiel 35–38
Bibliography: Hart (1990) fn. 14
Date: uncertain, but before A.D. 73
Significance: According to Hart, "In the majority of cases even the paragraph divisions are the same as those found in the Leningrad or Aleppo Codex."

MURABBA'AT

Name: (1)Mur Deut (= Mur2)
Content: Deuteronomy 10:1-3; 11:2-3; 12:25-26; 14:29–15:1 (or 15:2)
Bibliography: DJD 2
Date: Herodian
Significance: The text corresponds to the MT.

Name: (2)Mur Gen (= Mur1)
Content: Genesis 32:4-5, 30, 33 (=32)–33:1; 34:5-7, 30–35:1, 4-7
Bibliography: DJD 2
Date: probably no later than A.D. 132, the time of the Second Jewish Revolt.
Significance: The fragments of (2)Mur Gen, (2)Mur Exod, and (2)Mur Num are probably from the same scroll. The text is virtually identical to the MT.

Name: (2)Mur Exod (= Mur1)
Content: Exodus 4:28-31; 5:3; 6:5-11
Bibliography: DJD 2
Date: uncertain
Significance: See comments on (2)Mur Gen above.

Name: (2)Mur Num (= Mur1)
Content: Numbers 34:10; 36:7-11
Bibliography: DJD 2
Date: uncertain
Significance: See comments on (2)Mur Gen above.

Name: (2)Mur Isa (= Mur3)
Content: Isaiah 1:4-14

Bibliography: DJD 2
Date: first century A.D.
Significance: The text is identical to the MT.

Name: (2)Mur XII (= Mur88)
Content: Joel 2:20, 26-27; 3:1-5; 4:1-16; Amos 1:5-15; 2:1; 6:1; 7:3-16;
8:4-7, 11-14; 9:1-15; Obadiah 1-21; Jonah 1:1-16; 2:1-11; 3:1-10; 4:1-
11; Micah 1:1-16; 2:1-13; 3:1-12; 4:1-14; 5:1, 5-14; 6:1-7, 11-16; 7:1-
20; Nahum 1:1-14; 2:1-14; 3:1-19; Habakkuk 1:3-15; 2:5-10, 18-20;
3:1-19; Zephaniah 1:1, 11-18; 2:1-15; 3:1-20; Haggai 1:1-15; 2:1-6, 10,
12-23; Zechariah 1:1-4
Bibliography: DJD 2
Date: uncertain
Significance: The Minor Prophets scroll is by far the most extensively preserved and most important manuscript found at Murabba'at. The text is
almost identical to the MT. The *kethib* readings (i.e., the readings of the
text as opposed to the readings in the margin of the MT) at Obadiah 11
and Habakkuk 3:14 are supported here.

Name: Mur(?) Gen
Content: Genesis 33:18–34:3
Bibliography: Puech (1980)
Date: uncertain

NAHAL HEVER

Name: Hev(?) Gen
Content: Genesis 35:6-10; 36:5-12
Bibliography: *Annual of the Department of Antiquities of Jordan* 2;
Burchard (1966)
Date: no later than second century A.D.
Significance: The text is virtually identical to the MT.

Name: 5/6Hev Num
Content: Numbers 20:7-8
Bibliography: Yadin (1962)
Date: probably first century A.D.
Significance: The text of this very small fragment corresponds to the MT.

Name: 5/6Hev Ps
Content: Psalms 15:1-5; 16:1 (unconfirmed earlier identification: 7:14–
31:22)
Bibliography: Yadin (1962)
Date: c. A.D. 50–100
Significance: The text and orthography corresponds to the MT, except the
first phrase of the MT is absent here. In the MT there is no parallel to
this phrase.

Name: 8HevgkXII
Content: Jonah 1:14-16; 2:1-7; 3:2-5, 7-10; 4:1-2, 5; Micah 1:1-8; 2:7-9;

3:4-6; 4:3-5, 6-10; 5:1-4 (=2-5), 5-6; Nahum 1:13-14; 2:5-10, 13-14; 3:3, 6-17; Habakkuk 1:5-11, 14-17; 2:1-8, 13-20; 3:8-15; Zephaniah 1:1-6, 13-18; 2:9-10; 3:6-7; Zechariah 1:1-4, 12-15; 2:2-4, 6-12, 16-17 (=1:19–2:13); 3:1-2, 4-7; 8:19-21, 23; 9:1-5

Bibliography: DJD 8

Date: Opinions vary as to the dating of this manuscript. T. C. Skeat places it as early as the first century B.C. Others place it somewhere in the first century A.D. See DJD 8:19-26 for a full discussion of the work of the two scribes and the paleographic evidence for dating.

Significance: This Greek Minor Prophets scroll is one of the most significant finds among the Dead Sea Scrolls. On the basis of a careful study of the manuscript, Barthélemy (1963) concluded that we have here a Greek translation that was revised toward the MT along the lines seen in what is known as the *kaige* recension, named for the use of Greek *kaige* to represent the Hebrew direct object marker *'et*.

OTHER MANUSCRIPTS FOUND ELSEWHERE

Prior to the discovery of the Dead Sea Scrolls, several other manuscripts dating from the first century A.D. or earlier had been found. For example, the Nash Papyrus, mentioned earlier, is a valuable resource for the paleographic dating of the Dead Sea Scrolls. Several manuscripts of the Old Greek translation of the Old Testament provide an important witness to this ancient translation prior to the emergence of what became the standard Greek text of the Old Testament used by the Christian church. These manuscripts are described here to complete the picture of available manuscript evidence, although their textual evidence is not considered in any comprehensive manner.

Name: Nash Papyrus
Content: Exodus 20:2-17; Deuteronomy 6:4-5
Bibliography: Albright, BASOR 115 (1949):10-19
Date: c. 150 B.C.
Significance: The text of the Ten Commandments in the Nash papyrus is similar to the LXX text of Exodus 20. The Nash papyrus also includes the *Shema* from Deuteronomy 6:4-5 with the longer text of the LXX. The Nash Papyrus appears to be a biblical text designed for liturgical use. The combination of the Ten Commandments and the *Shema* was used in the Second Temple period (see Mishnah: Tamid 5:1, "they recited the Decalogue, the *Shema*, etc."). An important text such as the Ten Commandments existed in a form similar to the Hebrew text underlying the LXX translation. Compare 4QDeut[n].

Name: P. Ryl. Gk. 458 (= Rahlfs/Göttingen no. 957)
Content: Deuteronomy 23:24(26)–24:3; 25:1-3; 26:12, 17-19; 28:31-33

Bibliography: Roberts (1936), *Two Biblical Papyri in the John Rylands Library*.

Date: late second century B.C.

Name: Greek papyrus Fouad 266 (= Rahlfs/Göttingen nos. 942, 848, and 847)

Content: 942: Genesis 3:10-12; 4:5-7, 23; 7:17-20; 37:34-36; 38:1, 10-12.
848: portions of Deuteronomy 17–33.
847: portions of Deuteronomy 10, 11, 31–33.

Place of Discovery: Cairo

Bibliography: Zaki Aly and Ludwig Koenen, *Three Rolls of the Early Septuagint: Genesis and Deuteronomy* (Rudolf Habelt: 1980).

Date: c. 100 B.C.

Significance: The divine name is written in paleo-Hebrew letters.

Name: Silver Amulets

Content: Numbers 6:24-26

Place of Discovery: Ketef Hinnom, Jerusalem (1979)

Bibliography: Ada Yardeni, "Remarks on the Priestly Blessing on Two Ancient Amulets from Jerusalem." *Vetus Testamentum* 41 (1991):176-185. A detailed description, with plates and transcriptions, is given in an article written in modern Hebrew by Gabriel Barkay, "The Priestly Blessing on the Ketef Hinnom Plaques" (*Cathedra* 52 [1989]:37-76).

Date: late seventh or early sixth century B.C.

Significance: These tiny amulets on thin silver plaques contain the earliest known text of the Old Testament. They have been quite difficult to decipher, but definitely contain the text of the priestly blessing found in Numbers 6:24-26, "The LORD bless you and keep you . . . and give you peace." The extant portion of the Hebrew text of plaque 1 is identical to the MT. In plaque 2 there is an omission of a portion of the MT.

THE SHAPIRA MANUSCRIPT

In 1883, Moshe W. Shapira, an antiquities dealer from Jerusalem and Jewish convert to Christianity, offered to sell to the British Museum fifteen leather fragments containing portions of the book of Deuteronomy, including the Decalogue. The academic community of the day was initially quite interested in the document but ultimately ruled it a forgery, probably based in part on Shapira's tarnished reputation as an antiquities dealer. Distraught, Shapira committed suicide in 1884. The manuscript vanished and the entire Shapira matter was quickly forgotten until the discovery of the Dead Sea Scrolls. In the mid-1950s Menahem Mansoor reopened the question and suggested that the case for authenticity be reexamined (1959). John M. Allegro, one of the "official" Dead Sea Scroll editors, wrote a popular account of the Shapira affair, calling for a reexamination of its authenticity (1965). Despite these calls for reconsideration, there has been little further interest shown in Shapira's Deuteronomy.

On what basis did Mansoor and Allegro believe that the manuscript may not be a forgery? The rejection of authenticity was based on several arguments that no longer seem convincing in light of what we now know about paleography, scribal habits, and textual traditions. Since the manuscript is now lost, we can only examine the copy made by C. D. Ginsburg. At the time, the script was considered to be a forgery based on the writing style of the Moabite stone. We now know that numerous manuscripts at Qumran were written by imitating an archaic Hebrew style. The handwriting of Ginsberg's copy of the Shapira document is by no means identical to Qumran paleo-Hebrew, but it does show that the general style was used in some documents over a long period of time. The Shapira manuscript was written in short columns of about eight lines on narrow leather strips, a characteristic thought by Shapira's critics to demonstrate it as being not authentic. The biblical text itself differed editorially from the Masoretic Text, a phenomenon thought to be unlikely, especially for a text that included the Decalogue. Yet several Qumran manuscripts are written in short columns, including 4QDeut^n, which is a harmonistic text.

The question of the authenticity of the Shapira Deuteronomy can probably never be resolved, especially since the manuscript is now lost. Yet it remains an intriguing possibility that Shapira had indeed come into possession of an ancient scroll of Deuteronomy, perhaps even originally from the Dead Sea area.

CHART OF BIBLICAL MANUSCRIPTS
FROM THE DEAD SEA REGION

Contents of individual chapters are indicated by:

● = entire chapter
◑ = part of a chapter
○ = one verse only
◆ = part of a chapter, but exact content not yet published

GENESIS

	1 (1-5)	1 (6-10)	2 (1-5)	2 (6-10)	3 (1-5)	3 (6-10)	4 (1-5)	4 (6-10)	5 (1-5)	5 (6-10)
1Q	◑ ◑			◑◑◑						
2Q				◑			◑			
4Q[a]				◆	◆	◆◆	◆◆	◆◆	◆	◆◆◆◆
4Q[b]	◑◑	◑◑								
4Q[c]								○◑		
4Q[d]	◑									
4Q[e]							◆◆	◆ ◆◆◆		◆
4Q[f]										◑
4Q[g]	◑◑									
4Q[h]	◑									
4Q[j]								◆◆◆ ◆		
4Q[k]	◑◑◑									
4Qpaleo[l]										○
4Qpaleo[m]					◑					
6Qpaleo		◑								
8Q			◑							
Mas										◑
(2)Mur							◑○◑◑			
Mur(?)							◑◑			
?Hev						◑	◑			

	1		2		3		4	
	12345	67890	12345	67890	12345	67890	12345	67890
1Q			◐	◐◐ ◐				
2Q[a]	◐	◐ ◐	◐◐		◐	◐	◐	
2Q[b]		◐	◐	◐○ ◐◐	◐	◐ ○		
2Q[c]	◐							
4Q[a]	♦♦♦♦♦	♦♦♦♦						
4Q[b]	◐							
4Q[c]			◐					
4Q[d]			◐					
4Q[e]			◐					
4Q[f]								◐
4Q[g]			◐					
4Q[h]		◐						
4Q[j]								
4Q[k]								
4Qpaleo[l]	◐◐◐	◐◐◐	◐◐ ◐	◐◐◐◐◐	◐◐ ◐	◐◐	◐	
4Qpaleo[m]		◐◐◐◐◐	◐◐◐◐◐	◐◐◐◐◐	◐◐◐◐◐	◐◐◐◐◐	◐◐◐◐○	◐◐
4QDeut[j]			◐◐					
(2)Mur	◐◐	◐						
7QpapGr						◐		

LEVITICUS

	1		2			
	1 2 3 4 5	6 7 8 9 0	1 2 3 4 5	6 7 8 9 0	1 2 3 4 5	6 7
1Qpaleo			◐		◐◐	◐◐◐
2Qpaleo			◐			
4Qᵃ			◐	◐		◐
4Qᵇ	◐◐				◐◐◐◐	
4Qᶜ	◐					
4Qᵈ			◐◐	◐		
6Qpaleo		◐				
11Q		◐◐				
11Qpaleo	◐	◐	◐ ◐◐◐	◐◐◐◐◐	◐◐◐◐◐	◐◐
Masᵃ	◐					
Masᵇ		◆◆◆	◆◆			
4Qtg				◐		
4Qgkᵃ					◐	
4Qgkᵇ	○◐◐◐◐	◐				

NUMBERS

	1		2		3			
	1 2 3 4 5	6 7 8 9 0	1 2 3 4 5	6 7 8 9 0	1 2 3 4 5	6 7 8 9 0	1 2 3 4 5	6
1Qpaleo	◐							
2Qᵃ	◐◐							
2Qᵇ							◐	
2Qᶜ		○						
2Qᵈ?				◐				
4Qᵃ	◐◐◐◐◐	◐◐	◐○					
4Qᵇ			◐◐◐ ○	◐◐◐◐◐	◐◐◐◐◐	◐◐◐◐◐	◐◐◐◐◐	◐
(2) Mur							○	◐
5/6Hev				◐				
4Qgk	◐◐							

DEUTERONOMY

	1			2			3		
	1 2 3 4 5	6 7 8 9 0	1 2 3 4 5	6 7 8 9 0	1 2 3 4 5	6 7 8 9 0	1 2 3 4 5	6 7 8 9 0	1 2 3 4
1Q[a]	◐　◐	◐◐	◐　◐◐	◐					
1Q[b]	◐	◐○	◐　　◐	○	◐　◐◐		◐◐◐	◐◐◐	
2Q[a]	◐								
2Q[b]				◐					
2Q[c]		◐							
4Q[a]				○◐					
4Q[b]							◐◐	◐◐	
4Q[c]	◐◐	◐◐◐◐	◐◐◐　◐	◐◐◐			○◐◐◐	◐○	
4Q[d]	◐◐○								
4Q[e]	○	◐◐							
4Q[f]	◐	◐◐◐		◐◐◐◐	◐◐◐◐◐	◐◐			
4Q[g]		◐			◐◐◐	◐　◐			
4Q[h]	◐◐			○				◐　◐	
4Q[i]				◐　○◐◐◐					
4Q[j]	◐　◐　◐	◐					◐		
4Q[k]	◐	◐	◐◐	◐◐◐○	◐		◐		
4Q[l]	◐					◐◐	○　◐◐		
4Q[m]	◐◐	◐							
4Q[n]	◐○　◐								
4Q[o]	◐◐						◐◐		
4Q[p]		◐							
4Q[q]							◐		
4Qpaleo[r]	○	◐	◐◐○◐◐	◐	◐	◐　◐	◐◐◐○		
4Qpaleo[s]					◐				
5Q		◐◐◐							
6Qpap?					○				
4Qgk		◐							
Mas							◐◐		
(1) Mur		◐　◐◐　◐○							

90

JOSHUA

	1		2		
	1 2 3 4 5	6 7 8 9 0	1 2 3 4 5	6 7 8 9 0	1 2 3 4
4Q^a	◆◆◆◆	◐◐◐ ◐			
4Q^b	◐◐◐			◐	

JUDGES

	1		2		
	1 2 3 4 5	6 7 8 9 0	1 2 3 4 5	6 7 8 9 0	1
1Q		◐ ◯◐			
4Q^a		◐			
4Q^b				◐	◐

RUTH

	1 2 3 4
2Q^a	◐◐◐
2Q^b	◐
4Q^a	◆
4Q^b	◐

1 SAMUEL

	1		2		3		
	1 2 3 4 5	6 7 8 9 0	1 2 3 4 5	6 7 8 9 0	1 2 3 4 5	6 7 8 9 0	1 2
1Q				◐			
4Q^a	◐◐◐◐◐	◐◯◐◐◐	◐◐ ◐◐	◐		◐◐ ◐◐◐ ◐	◐
4Q^b				◐ ◐◐	◐ ◐		
4Q^c					◐		

2 SAMUEL

	1		2		
	1 2 3 4 5	6 7 8 9 0	1 2 3 4 5	6 7 8 9 0	1 2 3 4
1Q				◐ ◐ ◐	
4Q^a	◐◐◐◐	◐◐◐ ◐	◐◐◐◐◐ ◐	◐◐◐	◐◐◐◐
4Q^b					
4Q^c			◐◐		

1 KINGS

	1		2		
	1 2 3 4 5	6 7 8 9 0	1 2 3 4 5	6 7 8 9 0	1 2
4Q		◑◑			
5Q	◑				
6Qpap	◑		◑		◑

2 KINGS

	1		2		
	1 2 3 4 5	6 7 8 9 0	1 2 3 4 5	6 7 8 9 0	1 2 3 4 5
4Q					
5Q					
6Qpap	○	○◑◑◑◑			

1 CHRONICLES

	1		2			
	1 2 3 4 5	6 7 8 9 0	1 2 3 4 5	6 7 8 9 0	1 2 3 4 5	6 7 8 9
4Q						

2 CHRONICLES

	1		2		3			
	1 2 3 4 5	6 7 8 9 0	1 2 3 4 5	6 7 8 9 0	1 2 3 4 5	6 7 8 9 0	1 2 3 4 5	6
4Q						○◑		

EZRA

	1	
	1 2 3 4 5	6 7 8 9 0
4Q	◐○	◐

NEHEMIAH

	1		
	1 2 3 4 5	6 7 8 9 0	1 2 3
4Q			

ESTHER

	1	
	1 2 3 4 5	6 7 8 9 0

No portion of Esther found among the Dead Sea Scrolls

JOB

	1		2		3		4		
	1 2 3 4 5	6 7 8 9 0	1 2 3 4 5	6 7 8 9 0	1 2 3 4 5	6 7 8 9 0	1 2 3 4 5	6 7 8 9 0	1 2
2Q							◐		
4Qᵃ								◆	
4Qᵇ			◆						
4Qpaleoᶜ			◐◐						
4Qtg	◐◐◐								
11Qtg				◐◐◐◐ ◐◐ ◐◐	◐◐◐◐◐	◐◐◐◐◐	◐◐◐◐◐		◐◐

PSALMS / Book I

The following chart indicates which verses of Psalms (Book I, Pss. 1–41) are preserved in each manuscript. Filled symbols (◐) and open symbols (○) mark the relevant psalm columns.

MS	1	2	3	4	5	6	7	8	9	10	11	12	13	14	15	16	17	18	19	20	21	22	23	24	25	26	27	28	29	30	31	32	33	34	35	36	37	38	39	40	41
1Q^a																																									
1Q^b																																									
1Q^c																																									
2Q																																									
3Q		◐																																							
4Q^a					◐	◐																			◐						◐		◐	◐	◐	◐					
4Q^b																																									
4Q^c																◐		◐								◐	◐										◐		◐		
4Q^d																																									
4Q^e																																									
4Q^f																						◐																			
4Q^g																																									
4Q^h																																									
4Q^j																																									
4Q^k																																									
4Q^l																																									
4Q^m																																									
4Q^n																																									
4Q^o																																									
4Q^p																																									
4Q^q																															◐		◐	◐							
4Q^r																										◐	○			◐											
4Q^s					◐	○																																			
4Qfrg^1																																									
4Qfrg^2																																									
4Qfrg^3																																									
4QPs89																																									
5Q																																									
6Qpap																																									
8Q																	◐	◐																							
11Q^a																																									
11Q^b																																									
11Q^c		◐					◐				◐	◐	◐			◐	◐																								
11Q^{cS+}																																				◐	◐	◐	◐	◐	
11Q^d																																						◐	○		
11QAp^a																																									
Mas^a																																									
Mas^b																																									
5/6Hev															◐	○																									

PSALMS / Book II

Ms	42	43	44	45	46	47	48	49	50	51	52	53	54	55	56	57	58	59	60	61	62	63	64	65	66	67	68	69	70	71	72
1Q^a																															
1Q^b																															
1Q^c			◑																												
2Q																															
3Q																															
4Q^a						◑					◑	◑		○		○	◑								◑	◑		◑	◑		
4Q^b																															
4Q^c						◑		◑	◑	○	○	○																			
4Q^d																															
4Q^e																															
4Q^f																															
4Q^g																															
4Q^h																															
4Q^j						◑	◑																								
4Q^k																															
4Q^l																															
4Q^m																															
4Q^n																															
4Q^o																															
4Q^p																															
4Q^q																															
4Q^r																															
4Q^s																															
4Qfrg^1		○																													
4Qfrg^2																															
4Qfrg^3																															
4QPs89																															
5Q																															
6Qpap																															
8Q																															
11Q^a																															
11Q^b																															
11Q^c	◑																														
11Q^{cS+}																															
11Q^d	◑														◑						◑										
11QAp^a																															
Mas^a																															
Mas^b																															
5/6Hev																															

	7	8		9		1 0		
	3 4 5	6 7 8 9 0	1 2 3 4 5	6 7 8 9 0	1 2 3 4 5	6 7 8 9 0	1 2 3 4 5	6
1Q^a				◐	◐ ○◐○	○		
1Q^b								
1Q^c								
2Q							◐◐	
3Q								
4Q^a								
4Q^b					◐◐◐◐	○ ○◐◐	◐◐	
4Q^c								
4Q^d							◐	
4Q^e		◐◐◐	◐	◐ ◐◐			◐◐	
4Q^f								
4Q^g								
4Q^h								
4Q^j								
4Q^k								
4Q^l							◐	
4Q^m					◐ ◐	◐◐		
4Q^n								
4Q^o								
4Q^p								
4Q^q								
4Q^r								
4Q^s								
4Qfrg^1								
4Qfrg^2			○					
4Qfrg^3						○		
4QPs89				◐				
5Q								
6Qpap		◐						
8Q								
11Q^a							◐◐◐◐◐	
11Q^b								
11Q^c		◐○						
11Q^cS+								
11Q^d		◐	◐					
11QAp^a					◐			
Mas^a			◐◐◐◐◐					
Mas^b								
5/6Hev								

	10		11		12		13		14	15
	7 8 9 0	1 2 3 4 5	6 7 8 9 0	1 2 3 4 5	6 7 8 9 0	1 2 3 4 5	6 7 8 9 0	1 2 3 4 5	6 7 8 9 0	
1Q^a			◐							
1Q^b					○◐○					
1Q^c										
2Q										
3Q										
4Q^a										
4Q^b		◐○ ◐◐ ◐								
4Q^c										
4Q^d								?	◐◐	
4Q^e	○	◐◐	○	◐◐ ◐◐						
4Q^f	◐ ◐									
4Q^g			◐							
4Q^h			◐							
4Q^j										
4Q^k					◐					
4Q^l										
4Q^m										
4Q^n					◐○					
4Q^o		◐◐◐								
4Q^p								◐		
4Q^q										
4Q^r										
4Q^s										
4Qfrg^1										
4Qfrg^2										
4Qfrg^3										
4QPs89										
5Q			◐							
6Qpap										
8Q										
11Q^a	◐		◐◐	◐◐◐◐◐	◐○◐◐◐	○◐◐◐◐	◐◐◐◐◐	◐◐◐◐◐	◐◐◐◐◐	
11Q^b			◐		◐			○ ◐		
11Q^c										
11Q^cS+										
11Q^d										
11QAp^a										
Mas^a										
Mas^b									◐	
5/6Hev										

PROVERBS

	1		2		3		
	1 2 3 4 5	6 7 8 9 0	1 2 3 4 5	6 7 8 9 0	1 2 3 4 5	6 7 8 9 0	1
4Q[a]	◐○						
4Q[b]			◐◐				

ECCLESIASTES

	1		
	1 2 3 4 5	6 7 8 9 0	1 2
4Q[a]	◐	◐◐	
4Q[b]	◐		

SONG OF SOLOMON

	1 2 3 4 5	6 7 8
4Q[a]	◐◐	
4Q[b]	◐◐◐○	
4Q[c]		
6Q	◐	

ISAIAH

	1		2		3		4	
	1 2 3 4 5	6 7 8 9 0	1 2 3 4 5	6 7 8 9 0	1 2 3 4 5	6 7 8 9 0	1 2 3 4 5	6 7 8 9 0
1Q^a	◑◑●●◑	◑◑◑◑◑	●●●●●	●●●●●	●●●●●	●●●●●	●●●●●	●●●●●
1Q^b		◑○ ◑	◑◑ ◑◑	◑ ◑○	◑◑◑◑	◑ ◑◑◑	◑	◑◑◑◑
4Q^a	◑◑ ◑	◑	◑◑◑	◑ ◑◑	◑◑◑			
4Q^b	◑◑◑ ◑	◑	◑◑○	◑◑◑◑	◑◑ ○	◑	◑	◑◑ ◑◑
4Q^c		◑◑	◑○ ◑		○◑◑◑◑	◑	◑	
4Q^d								
4Q^e		◑◑◑						
4Q^f	◑◑ ◑	◑◑◑		◑	◑ ◑	◑◑		
4Q^g								
4Q^h		◑◑						
4Q^j	◑							
4Q^k						◑◑		
4Q^l	◑	◑	◑◑◑◑					
4Q^m		◑						
4Q^n								
4Q^o			◑○ ◑					
4Qpap^p	◑							
4Q^q								
4Q^r								
5Q								◑
(2) Mur	◑							

	5		6			
	1 2 3 4 5	6 7 8 9 0	1 2 3 4 5	6 7 8 9 0	1 2 3 4 5	6
1Q^a	●●●●◑	●●●●●	●●●●●	●●●●●	●●●●●	◑
1Q^b	◑ ◑◑◑	◑◑◑◑◑	◑◑◑◑◑	◑◑◑◑◑	◑◑◑◑◑	◑
4Q^a						
4Q^b	◑ ◑◑◑	◑ ◑	◑◑◑		◑ ◑○	○
4Q^c	◑	◑ ◑	◑◑◑◑◑			◑
4Q^d		◑◑◑◑	◑◑◑	◑◑		
4Q^e						
4Q^f						
4Q^g	◑◑					
4Q^h	◑			◑◑ ◑◑	◑	
4Q^j						
4Q^k						
4Q^l						
4Q^m						
4Q^n				◑		
4Q^o						
4Qpap^p						
4Q^q			◑			
4Q^r						
5Q						
(2) Mur						

100

JEREMIAH

	1 (1-5)	1 (6-10)	2 (1-5)	2 (6-10)	3 (1-5)	3 (6-10)
2Q						
4Qᵃ		●●●●	●●●●●	●●●	●	
4Qᵇ		●●				
4Qᶜ	●	●●●		●●	●● ● ●● ●	
4Qᵈ (Tov)						
4Qᵉ (Tov)						

JEREMIAH (continued)

	4 (1-5)	4 (6-10)	5 (1-5)	5 (6-10)	1 2
2Q			●●●	●●●●	
4Qᵃ					
4Qᵇ					
4Qᶜ	◆ ◆				
4Qᵈ (Tov)			●		
4Qᵉ (Tov)				●	

LAMENTATIONS

	1 2 3 4 5
3Q	● ●
4Q	●
5Qᵃ	●●
5Qᵇ	●

EZEKIEL

	1 (1-5)	1 (6-10)	2 (1-5)	2 (6-10)	3 (1-5)	3 (6-10)	4 (1-5)	4 (6-10)	(1-5)	678
1Q	●○									
3Q			●							
4Qᵃ		●	● ●		●			●		
4Qᵇ	●									
4Qᶜ					●					
11Q	●● ● ○									
Mas							● ●●●			

101

DANIEL

	1 2 3 4 5	6 7 8 9 0	1 2
1Q^a	●●		
1Q^b	●		
4Q^a	●●●●●	●● ●	●
4Q^b	●	●●●	
4Q^c		●	●
4Q^d			
4Q^e			
6Qpap		● ●	●

MINOR PROPHETS (part 1)
Hosea   Joel   Amos

	Hosea			Joel	Amos	
	1 2 3 4 5	6 7 8 9 0	1 2 3 4	1 2 3 4	1 2 3 4 5	6 7 8 9
4Q^a						
4Q^b						
4Q^c	●●●●		●●	●● ●	●●●	●●
4Q^d	●●					
4Q^e						
4Q^f						
4Q^g						
4Q^?			●●			
5Q					●	
7Q5						
(2) Mur				●●●	●○	○●●●
8HevGk						

102

MINOR PROPHETS (part 2)

	Ob	Jonah	Micah		Nah	Hab
	x	1 2 3 4	1 2 3 4 5	6 7	1 2 3	1 2 3
4Q^a		◐○○				
4Q^b						
4Q^c						
4Q^d						
4Q^e						
4Q^f		◐	◐			
4Q^g						
4Q$^?$						
5Q						
7Q5						
(2) Mur	◐	◐◐◐◐	◐◐◐◐◐	◐◐	◐◐◐	◐◐◐
8HevGk		◐◐◐◐	◐◐◐◐◐		◐◐◐	◐◐◐

MINOR PROPHETS (part 3)

	Zeph	Hag	Zech			Mal
				1		
	1 2 3	1 2	1 2 3 4 5	6 7 8 9 0	1 2 3 4	1 2 3
4Q^a					○	◐◐
4Qb	◐◐◐	◐◐				
4Q^c	○◐					◐
4Q^d						
4Q^e		◐	◐◐◐◐◐	◐	◐	
4Q^f						
4Q^g						
5Q						
7Q5				◐		
(2) Mur	◐◐◐	◐◐	◐			
(Hev)	◐◐◐		◐◐◐	◐◐		

PART THREE

THE EFFECT OF THE DEAD SEA SCROLLS ON MODERN TRANSLATIONS OF THE OLD TESTAMENT

The number of Old Testament manuscripts among the Dead Sea Scroll discoveries (180) is nearly twice that of New Testament Greek papyri (96), and the Dead Sea manuscripts are nearly 1,000 years older than Hebrew Bible manuscripts known before 1947 (the beginning date for the scroll discoveries). However, most people will be surprised to learn that there are relatively few passages in modern English translations of the Old Testament that have been affected by this manuscript evidence.

A number of factors account for this apparent undervaluation of the Dead Sea manuscripts. First, the majority of the manuscripts are quite fragmentary, but this can be said about the New Testament Greek papyri as well, with a few notable exceptions. Second, the pace of publication of the scrolls has been very slow, but this is much less true of the biblical manuscripts than of the sectarian documents from Qumran Cave 4. In fact, virtually all of the biblical manuscripts have been published in at least some preliminary form. It must also be kept in mind that many of the Dead Sea manuscripts preserve a text quite close to that of the Hebrew text underlying the Masoretic Text. In such cases, it can be argued that the Dead Sea manuscripts lend support to existing translation traditions that rely heavily on the Masoretic Text. Finally, we must recognize that the evaluation of the wealth of new evidence from the Dead Sea area has been a lengthy process. This is quite understandable, and in fact necessary, since the crucial period of the first centuries before and after Christ were previously so lacking in Hebrew manuscript evidence.

The understanding that now seems to be emerging about the textual situation of this period recognizes the existence of a variety of text types, among which existed one text type that was more stable than others— namely, the text we now know as the Masoretic Text. Existing side by side with this text (even within the same religious community, such as Qumran) were other texts, some of which show greater affinity with the

Hebrew text underlying the Septuagint, and others of which agree with many of the nonsectarian features of the Samaritan Pentateuch, and still others of which that show affinities with other traditions.

All these factors must be kept in mind when assessing the Dead Sea Scroll evidence in modern translations. The translations that were first able to take advantage of the new evidence understandably utilized it as evidence for a better or earlier textual witness, without first being able to assess the nature of the textual witness as a whole. More recent translations have now been able to benefit from a more comprehensive evaluation of the textual evidence and have sometimes made different textual decisions.

The following section contains all the passages from Genesis to Malachi in which the Dead Sea Scrolls have had a significant influence on modern translations of the Old Testament. The translations involved in this analysis are discussed in part one (pages 27-34).

GENESIS
Genesis 1:9
Translations generally render "into one place" to describe the gathering of the water. NAB, however, translates "into a single basin." The supplementary list of textual notes found in a few early printings of the NAB says that their translation is based on 4QGen and LXX. 4QGen[h] reads *mqwh* (basin) for MT *mqwm* (place). This Qumran reading suggests that the OG *sunagogen* (gathering place) had a Hebrew text that read *mqwh*. This variant reading may be appealing, especially in view of "dome" (for the more traditional "firmament") in verses 6 and 7. It should also be kept in mind that the OG *sunagogen* means "a gathering place" without necessarily referring to something as specific as a basin. For example, NJB translates "into a single mass," citing only the Greek text in support of their rendering. While *mqwh* is a more probable *Vorlage* than *mqwm,* it is not an absolute certainty. The textual critic must be aware of the translation technique of the ancient translator in order to assess the degree of probability of a particular Hebrew *Vorlage*. In this case, the discovery of 4QGen[h] provides relatively certain evidence that the Hebrew text used by the OG translator differed from the MT. But this evidence in itself does not settle the issue of which text is "better" or "earlier." HOTTP recommends that translators follow the MT.

EXODUS

Exodus 1:5

Is the number of Jacob's descendants "seventy" or "seventy-five"? 4QExod[b], together with the OG, reads "seventy-five." This Qumran reading was one of the examples Cross (1961) gave to demonstrate the existence of a Hebrew text that was closely related to the Egyptian (= OG) text type. It would seem at first glance that the translator simply needs to decide between the MT and the OG textual tradition. Translators have followed the MT, using "seventy," with some translations such as NIV and NEB adding a footnote with the alternate reading based on Qumran and Greek evidence. Surprisingly, HOTTP, which generally recommends translators follow the MT, prefers "seventy-five." The NIV reminds us that Stephen used "seventy-five" in his speech recorded in Acts 7:14. This is not altogether surprising, since Stephen quotes Amos 5:25-27 from the OG text type.

In Genesis 46:20 the OG includes the names of Joseph's three grandsons and two great-grandsons, increasing the total to "seventy-five" in Genesis 46:27. HOTTP believes that changes from original "seventy-five" to "seventy" in MT were triggered by a pious scribe who changed Deuteronomy 32:8 from "sons of God" to "sons of Israel" for theological reasons. A Qumran manuscript does read "sons of God" in Deuteronomy 32:8 (see the discussion below). HOTTP suggests that this change necessitated other textual changes in Genesis 46 and Exodus 1:5. If one is persuaded that the change in Deuteronomy 32:8 influenced the other changes, then a translation should follow the OG readings, some of which have additional Qumran support, in all related passages.

Exodus 9:28

The NEB mentions in a footnote that a scroll and the Septuagint add "and fire" after the words "thunder and hail." This is the reading in 4QExod[a] and most Septuagint manuscripts. It is rather surprising that NEB chooses to footnote only this textual variant in 4QExod[a], even though this manuscript shows several other agreements with OG. The REB drops the note.

Exodus 22:14 (22:13 in Hebrew text)

NEB and REB add "a beast" to the text, citing "Scroll" support for this addition that specifies what a man is borrowing from his neighbor. NRSV and NJB also add "an animal" to the text, but without a textual note. The Qumran manuscript evidence for "a beast" is found in 4Q158, a biblical paraphrase, not a copy of the book of Exodus. The fact that NRSV and NJB supply "an animal" without a textual note and that an ancient paraphrase supplies the word demonstrate that this is probably not a true textual variant but an effort by translators or the author of the paraphrase to make explicit what is implicit in the text. Thus, it is reasonable to conclude that this reading in 4Q158 is not a true textual variant.

It is rather surprising that only a few Qumran readings in the book of Exodus are cited by recent translators. Even the few that are considered are unimportant, except for Exodus 1:5. This underutilization is especially striking in view of the fact that there were fifteen copies of Exodus found at Qumran. Forty-five consecutive columns of 4QpaleoExod^m, out of a probable fifty-seven for the entire book, are partially preserved in this very important manuscript.

NUMBERS

Most of the copies of Numbers found in the Dead Sea area are quite fragmentary. With one notable exception, these fragments seem to support the MT. Thus, it is hardly surprising that no recent translation cites any of these manuscripts. The exceptional Numbers manuscript is 4QNum^b, which has only recently been published by Jastram in his dissertation (1990). Translators will need to await further evaluation of this manuscript, which shows a remarkable mixture of textual traditions (see pp. 59-60).

DEUTERONOMY

Deuteronomy 5:5

There is broad support in the ancient versions for the plural "words of the LORD," instead of MT's "word." 4QDeut^n also has plural *dbry YHWH* (words of the LORD). Other passages related to the Ten Commandments have the plural "words." The MT singular *dbr YHWH* (word of the LORD) can readily be explained as a case of haplography because of the adjacent *yod*s. On the other hand, the singular *dbr YHWH* can be understood as a plural construct written defectively. Thus, the net result is the same for the sake of translation, but the Qumran evidence lends support to interpreting the word as plural, which is also confirmed by the Samaritan Pentateuch and the ancient versions.

Deuteronomy 10:13

The NRSV adds "your God" to the familiar phrase "keep the command-ments of the Lord," citing Qumran, as well as Greek and Syriac, evidence. The addition of "your God" in the ancient versions is not surprising in light of the fact that this is the form of the phrase used elsewhere in the OT. The Qumran evidence comes from several phylacteries: 4Q128 (phylactery[A]), 4Q138 (phylactery[K]), and XQPhyl[1] (X here indicates that it is not known which Qumran cave this manuscript came from). Phylacteries are small receptacles containing selected verses from Exodus and Deuteronomy that were worn on the forehead and arm during prayer. Since the text of phylac-teries could be copied from memory, there was a tendency to harmonize and expand the text. This, in fact, is a general characteristic of the Qumran phy-lacteries. In textual criticism, harmonization explains the rise of a textual variant; it does not always provide evidence for an original reading. It is somewhat unusual, therefore, that NRSV chose to follow a textual variant found only in phylacteries, against the testimony of several ancient versions.

Deuteronomy 24:14

The NEB and REB follow 1QDeut[b] in the text, translating "You shall not keep back the wages of a man" instead of the reading of the MT: "You shall not oppress a hired man." Several ancient versions, including OG and Syriac, seem to support the Qumran text. The difference between the MT and Qumran is only one letter, *yod.* 1QDeut[b] reads *skr,* which would be vocalized as a noun, *sakar* ("wages"). The MT adds a *yod,* vocalized *sakir,* a related noun meaning "hired laborer," that is, one who earns wages. There is little difference in meaning, and this is why it is not cer-tain if the ancient versions reflect a Hebrew text corresponding to 1QDeut[b] or are reflecting the needs of their receptor language. The failure of the NEB and REB to cite versional evidence may support the latter view. However, HOTTP recommends "wages" as the preferred reading, but does not cite Qumran evidence for the Hebrew text.

Deuteronomy 31:1

The NJV, in one of only a few of textual notes in the Pentateuch, offers the variant of 1QDeut[b], supported by the Septuagint, in a footnote, "When Moses had finished speaking . . ." The NEB, REB, and NRSV adopt this Qumran reading for the text. It provides a smoother transition from the end of Moses' covenant-renewal speech to his final personal comments, in which he explains that the leadership will be handed over to Joshua.

Deuteronomy 32:8

Skehan (1954:12) found a small fragment that he thinks may be from a paraphrase or prose version of the Song of Moses. It may have been written by the same scribe of 4QDeut[q], but is clearly not from the same manuscript. The fragment of Deut 32:8 provides evidence for the non-MT reading "sons of God," and is cited as evidence for the translation in the text of the NEB and REB. The NIV mentions this textual variant in a footnote.

Deuteronomy 32:43

4QDeut[q] offers a number of textual variants from the MT that have influenced the NEB and NRSV translation of this verse. This fragment contains the last verses of the Song of Moses. It is significant that the manuscript ends with the last verse of the song and does not continue with the text of Deuteronomy 32:44ff. The manuscript also has a very wide outside margin with no evidence that any other manuscript panel was stitched to it. Based on this evidence, it is reasonable to conclude that 4QDeut[q] may have been a copy of the Song of Moses, rather than a copy of the book of Deuteronomy. This is not unusual in view of the importance and likely popularity of the song.

Even though the manuscript is a reliable witness, it should be borne in mind that there may have been a greater degree of scribal freedom in this type of document. The NRSV follows 4QDeut[q] in translating "heavens" for "nations," "children" for "servants," and the addition "worship him all you gods." (The NIV cites this addition in a footnote and translates "and let all the angels worship him.") All these variants are supported by evidence from the OG.

Deuteronomy 33:8

The NRSV, continuing the textual base of RSV, adds "to Levi." The RSV based its translation on the OG alone, while NRSV cites Qumran evidence; but it is not at all clear what specific Qumran manuscript the NRSV is referring to.

Deuteronomy 33:17

The NRSV follows 1QDeut[b], with support from the Samaritan Pentateuch and ancient versions, which lacks the third person, masculine, singular, pronoun suffix, *waw,* thereby producing the reading, "a firstborn bull," instead of "his firstborn bull" found in the MT. This is a case where the RSV translators had not followed the evidence of the ancient versions, but the supporting Qumran evidence seems to have tipped the scales in favor of the variant recently adopted by the NRSV revisers.

An examination of the photograph of fragment 20 of 1QDeut[b], published in DJD I, shows how difficult it sometimes is to evaluate manuscript evidence. In this case, only a few specks of ink remain of the Hebrew word for "bull," and the evidence for the missing *waw* in the text is based on the size of the space between extant words at the bottom of the fragment.

JOSHUA

Two copies of the book of Joshua were found at Qumran, both in Cave 4. As yet no translation has utilized the limited evidence attested by these fragments. There are significant differences between the MT and Old Greek in the book of Joshua, differences which, according to Tov (1986:337), are best accounted for as representing two different *editions* of the book, rather than only textual variants. Tov considers the generally longer MT edition a later development of an earlier edition reflected in the Old Greek and supported, in part, by some Qumran evidence. If this is true, how should translators utilize this textual evidence? If the Old Greek evidence is followed, with or without Qumran support, a basic question must first be settled: Are we seeking to reconstruct, with both textual and literary evidence, (1) the text of the book of Joshua *prior* to the Old Greek edition, (2) the text underlying the Old Greek as the earliest attested edition, or (3) the MT, which was the edition accepted in the Jewish canon? To ask the question in this way presupposes the acceptance of Tov's view of the textual history of the book of Joshua. Other views are, of course, possible. But we must now look at the question in an entirely new light since the Dead Sea Scroll evidence has come to the fore. Ultimately, translations may be affected less in the textual details of individual passages than in some of the larger issues of textual history and development.

JUDGES

Three copies of Judges were found at Qumran. The omission of "and their camels" in Judges 6:5 by 4QJdg[a] has not been followed by any recent translation. Older translations did not take notice of this variant either, since the only witness prior to the Qumran discoveries was the Old Latin. This reading may lend support to the theory, advanced by some scholars, that there was an Old Latin translation made directly from the Hebrew, perhaps antedating the Christian era, although it is dangerous to make any generalizations on such slender evidence.

RUTH

Four copies of Ruth were found at Qumran. It appears that these copies support the MT, although only preliminary information is available for the two copies found in Cave 4.

1 AND 2 SAMUEL

The complexity of the textual traditions of the books of Samuel has presented one of the major challenges in the study of Old Testament textual criticism. Other books, such as Jeremiah, exist in two different forms, one represented by the MT and the other by the Old Greek; and textual scholars have generally decided that either the MT or Old Greek represents the better edition, textually speaking. The textual situation in Samuel is more complex because MT is at times shorter and at other times longer than Old Greek. The Greek version, which we now have in the Septuagint, varies section by section in both translation technique and in textual tradition. With the discovery of several copies of Samuel, the most extensively preserved and most important of which is 4QSam[a], we now have another witness to the text of Samuel. Important early studies of 4QSam[a], such as Ulrich (1978), pointed out the fact that this manuscript shared many readings with the Old Greek tradition and even contained some additions that were earlier known only in the history of the Jewish monarchy written by Josephus in his *Antiquities*. Tov (1980) emphasizes the diversity of the textual traditions found in the variants in 4QSam[a], without denying the fact that 4QSam[a] lends strong support for many Old Greek readings.

Another aspect of Samuel textual studies is the fact that for many passages a parallel version exists in the book of Chronicles. On occasion, 4QSam[a] agrees with Chronicles, raising the possibility that some Chronicles additions and variants may have actually been known to the chronicler from a text of Samuel-Kings, rather than part of his retelling of the history of the monarchy. See Goshen-Gottstein (1988) and Martin (1984) for two general overviews of the text of Samuel. Tov (1980) and Barthélemy, *et al.* (1986) are collections of important studies of the text of Samuel, especially in light of the Dead Sea Scrolls. Pisano (1984) studies in great detail the significant pluses and minuses in the Masoretic, Old Greek, and Qumran texts, and generally prefers the MT.

Prior to the discovery of the Samuel manuscripts from Qumran, some translations, recognizing the textual problems in the book, utilized the Old Greek evidence. For example in 1 Samuel 10:1, the RSV includes the plus [1] ". . . over his people Israel? And you shall reign over the people of the LORD and you will save them from the hand of their enemies round about. And this shall be the sign to you that the LORD had anointed you to be prince. . . ." The text continues with "over," the same word at the beginning of the plus. The translators, agreeing with most scholars, believed that this large plus had dropped out because of haplography, that is, the scribe's eye dropped directly from the first "over" to the second, skipping the intermediate text. This phenomenon occurs elsewhere in Samuel. (The terms "plus" and "minus" are used instead of "addition" and "deletion," or similar terms in order not to prejudge whether a particular plus or minus was original or the result of a scribal change, whether inadvertent or intentional.)

Now that 4QSam[a], and to a lesser extent 4QSam[b,c], lend support to the pluses of the Old Greek, some translations have now included more Old Greek pluses even where the 4Q Samuel texts are no longer extant, since the translators have concluded that there was an early Hebrew text similar to the Old Greek text. The NAB and NRSV include the longer text of the Old Greek in 1 Samuel 4:1; 13:15; 14:23-24; and 29:10. The NAB alone also adds the Old Greek plus in 2 Sam 24:14. The Old Greek pluses that also have Qumran support are discussed below.

1 Samuel 1–2

These chapters contain the account of the birth and early life of Samuel. The NRSV contains twenty-seven textual notes in these two chapters; the

115

translation departs from the MT in all cases, with Qumran support for seventeen departures from the MT. The NAB has about the same number of departures from the MT. How does one account for this textual situation? Bo Johnson (1977) has suggested that the heart of the problem may lie in the fact that an authoritative Samuel scroll suffered damage or severe wear near the beginning of the scroll, a situation that is not uncommon in scrolls. A scribe then may have cautiously corrected the defective Vorlage as best he could, smoothing out the context where possible.

A more recent suggestion to explain the differences between the MT and the OG text of 1 Samuel 1 has been made by Stanley Walters (1988). He believes there are actually two stories of Hannah, one found in the MT and the other in the OG, similar to the way the Synoptic Gospel writers narrate the same incident in the life of Jesus, with a different focus and emphasis in line with the focus of each individual Gospel writer. The Old Greek versions add emphasis to the fact that Anna (the form of her name in Old Greek) was childless, while the MT points to the abuse Hannah suffered from the rival wife. In the MT Hannah was a participant in the presentation of the sacrifice the couple presented at Shiloh, while the OG specifies Elkanah. In the MT verse 24 ends with the curious phrase, "and the lad was a lad," leading some textual scholars to conclude that an entire line (or more) has dropped out of the MT due to the repetition of "lad." Added to this double witness of the story of Hannah and the birth of Samuel we now have the text of 4QSam[a], which generally supports the Old Greek. What is the translator to do? Walters says that "we should not treat the MS evidence—the MT, the versions, and Qumran—as if it were a card file of variant readings. . . . In 1 Samuel 1 there are two stories and not one . . . that must not be lost by collapsing these narratives into each other" (410-412). This is not to say that either version, the MT or the OG, is not without textual corruption. In fact, 1 Samuel 1:24 in the MT contains a textual problem, *befarim sheloshah* "three bulls," which most modern translations, including GNB, NAB, NIV, NRSV, REB, as well as HOTTP correct to "a three-year old bull," on the basis of Old Greek and Qumran evidence. In addition to this widely accepted correction, the NRSV translators also conjectured, on the basis of evidence from Old Greek and Qumran, that Hannah's promise to dedicate Samuel as a Nazirite is expanded in both verses 11 and 22: "He shall drink neither wine nor intoxicants" is prefixed to the promise in verse 11 that "no razor shall touch his head." In verse 22 "I will offer him as a Nazirite for all times" is added to Hannah's statement.

The NAB also includes these statements as well as other pluses of the OG, with Qumran support, such as "After the boy's father had sacrificed the young bull . . ." (1:25). The NAB chooses to follow some but not all of the Old Greek readings and Qumran supported pluses in chapter 1, contrary to the recommendation of Walters and Ulrich (1988:115). Most other translations follow the MT in its focus, although they are willing to correct an obvious error such as "three bulls."

1 Samuel 1:28 and 2:20

These verses contain related textual variants. In 1:28 the Old Greek says "She [Anna] left him [Samuel] there for the LORD." 4QSam^a probably contains a similar text, instead of the MT, "He [Elkanah] worshiped the LORD there." If the account in chapter 1 ends with a focus on Hannah's act of dedication, then the blessing of Eli in 2:20, according to Old Greek and 4QSam^a, logically follows, "May the Lord repay [instead of the MT 'give'] you with children by this woman for the gift that she made [instead of the MT 'the petition that she asked'] of the Lord." If translators believe that the Qumran and the OG version of the narrative is superior, then it follows that variants in both verses should be followed. This is what both the NRSV and NAB did, which is not at all surprising, since this is their preference for the opening chapters of Samuel.

1 Samuel 2:1

Based on the OG, with apparent support from 4QSam^a, the NAB omits "Hannah prayed." The omission provides a smooth transition from the events of chapter 1 to the text of Hannah's prayer. The NAB and NRSV translate "my victory" for "your victory" in the same verse, based on the Qumran evidence from the same manuscript.

1 Samuel 2:8

This verse contains an example of a large addition found in 4QSam^a, the text of which is poorly preserved. The Old Greek lacks this plus, as does the MT, although the two texts are not identical in content here. The NRSV places the 4QSam^a plus in a footnote, and the NAB incorporates it in the text, although because of the uncertainty of portions of the text in the poorly preserved fragment, the renderings are not identical. There is an even longer plus in 4QSam[a] in 2:10, which can be inferred only from the fact that there is room for four additional lines in the manuscript. The Old Greek also has a large plus here, but it is difficult to know if it corresponds to 4QSam[a]. No translation follows or even calls attention to this poorly preserved plus.

1 Samuel 2:21
The textual variants in verse 20 (see the discussion above) may relate to the variant in the opening word of 2:21 as well. Both the NAB and NRSV follow the 4QSam[a] reading, "And the LORD took note of Hannah," instead of the MT, "When the LORD took note of Hannah." The NJV also mentions this variant in a note.

1 Samuel 2:27-33
The NRSV follows six short 4QSam[a] readings in these verses, all with Old Greek support. In verse 27 the MT lacks "slaves," the omission of which may have be caused by the similar ending of the word before "slaves." The verse comments on the Israelites' sojourn in Egypt when they were slaves to the house of Pharaoh (NRSV). Without "slaves," the text is similar in meaning, but most descriptions of the Israelites' situation in Egypt describes them as slaves.

1 Samuel 3:4
Ulrich (1978:63) says, "One cannot say definitely whether 4QSam[a] had a second Samuel . . . but there is room for it." The NRSV reads "Samuel! Samuel!" and cites both Qumran and Old Greek. In this they follow RSV, which cites only the Old Greek evidence, but also points out that "Samuel" is repeated in 3:10. The translator must decide whether it is more likely that the best text contained a stylistic difference between 3:4 and 3:10, which a scribe later harmonized, or one occurrence of Samuel inadvertently dropped out of verse 4. Most translations prefer the former option.

1 Samuel 5:8-9
There are several textual variants in these verses relating to the movement of the ark to Gath. The NRSV and NAB follow 4QSam[a], which seems to

118

be somewhat smoother in style than the MT, but the essential meaning of the passage is not changed.

1 Samuel 5:11

Ulrich (1978:124) points out that "the translation of [O]G, with a Vorlage similar to 4Q, declined on theological grounds to translate 'the panic of the LORD,' and simply omitted *YHWH* [the divine name]." In a footnote, the NRSV points out that 4QSam[a] includes "LORD."

1 Samuel 6:3

The NRSV follows 4QSam[a] with "and will be ransomed," versus the MT, "and it will be known to you" (see Ulrich 1978:75-76). The NAB, the other modern translation that utilized the Samuel Qumran evidence extensively, does not do so here.

1 Samuel 9:24

This contains another minor 4QSam[a] variant that NRSV alone follows: "it is set before you," for the MT, "it was kept before you." The Qumran reading is smoother in the context.

1 Samuel 10:26

The word *chayil* in the MT is difficult to translate in this context. The NJV utilizes the evidence of 4QSam[a], supported by Old Greek, which reads *bene chayil*, to explain the meaning as "upstanding men," literally, "sons of strength/uprightness." Both the Qumran manuscripts and the ancient versions at times provide evidence that the ancient scribes and translators faced difficulties in understanding obscurities in the Hebrew text before them.

1 Samuel 10:27–11:1

Chapter 11 in the MT tells the story of how Nahash the Ammonite troubled the men of Jabesh. Nahash was willing to leave them alone if they submitted to having everyone's right eye gouged out. The MT offers no background information on the reason for Nahash's cruel requirement. However, 4QSam[a] offers an extended explanation: Nahash had already done this to the Gadites and the Reubenites. The historian, Josephus, also knew about Nahash's cruel practice, as described in his *Antiquities* 6.5.1 (6.68-71 in the Loeb edition of Josephus). The NRSV and NAB include this additional information in their translations. Although Nahash's pattern of cruelty was known from the works of Josephus, before the Qumran discovery, there was no evidence that this information was ever included in the actual biblical text. Now that 4QSam[a] contains this addition, some translators were persuaded that it could rightly find its place in the Bible.

A text that contains the long addition begins 11:1 with a narrative sequence statement, "About a month later." Naturally, versions that include the previous addition will also include this reading. Both REB and NEB follow the same variant, the latter only on the basis of the Old Greek evidence.

1 Samuel 11:8

According to the MT, Saul mustered an army of thirty thousand from Judah, but according to 4QSam[a] the number was seventy thousand. The NRSV translators chose to follow the higher number in the Qumran manuscript, probably because the translators thought that 4QSam[a] preserved many superior readings in Samuel. On the other hand, there is no compelling reason to prefer the higher number. Inflating numbers is a tendency frequently seen in later versions and texts.

1 Samuel 17–18

These chapters tell the story of David and Goliath. A review of the NRSV and NAB shows that no Qumran variants are considered, since only a very few fragments of these chapters survive in two manuscripts, 1QSam and 4QSam[a]. However, there are major and significant differences between the MT and OG accounts. The complex textual relationships are the subject of an entire book by Barthélemy, *et al.* (1986). Ulrich (1988:115) believes that the best textual witness is found in the OG, even though he prefers the MT for other portions of Samuel. On the other hand, Gooding (in Barthélemy 1986) defends the superiority of the longer MT account. Although there is little help from Qumran here, a careful study of the existing textual traditions has implications for the value of Qumran witnesses for the rest of Samuel.

1 Samuel 20:29-38

In these ten verses the NAB diverges from the MT eight times, citing 4QSam[b]. However, the extant fragments of chapter 20 from 4QSam[b] are not included in the preliminary edition of Cross (1955) or later studies such as Andersen and Freedman (1989). The variants are discussed in McCarter (1980). He includes a detailed discussion of all the Qumran Samuel variants in his commentaries (1980, 1984).

1 Samuel 21:2

The MT is difficult to translate here. 4QSam[b], with support from the OG, makes the meaning more clear and is followed in the NRSV text and cited in a note in the NJV. In cases such as these, it is sometimes difficult to determine whether Q and OG witness a better and older text or whether they are resolving a difficulty.

1 Samuel 23:11

Although there are a number of examples of minuses in the MT of Samuel that translators have considered omissions by haplography and have, accordingly, followed Qumran evidence, this verse contains the MT plus that NRSV and NAB omit on the evidence of 4QSam[b].

1 Samuel 23:14, 16

4QSam[b] has *Yhwh* "the Lord," instead of the MT *Elohim* "God." In verse 16 it is possible that 4QSam[b] also has *Yhwh,* but only a part of the last letter has survived. The NAB and NRSV translate "the LORD," although there are a number of cases of the alternation of "the Lord" and "God" in the textual witnesses to the Old Testament.

2 Samuel 6:1-16

This section parallels portions of 1 Chronicles 13, 15, and 16. Naturally, the parallel accounts of the return of the ark of the covenant creates the possibility of harmonizations between the two accounts. Ulrich has discussed the complex interrelationships of the textual variants found in 4QSam[a], the MT, OG, and Josephus in this chapter (1978:194-197). A survey of NRSV, NAB, and NIV demonstrates that the translators relied on the Qumran evidence, with occasional support coming from ancient Greek manuscripts and parallels in 1 Chronicles.

2 Samuel 12:6

The 4QSam[a] addition of "in sackcloth" is included in the text of the REB and quoted in a note in the NJV, but not cited at all by the NRSV.

2 Samuel 13:21

The long addition found in 4QSam^a and in the OG is included in the text of the NRSV.

2 Samuel 13:27

The NRSV includes the Old Greek plus and mentions the evidence of 4QSam^a.

2 Samuel 18:11

The NAB translates the 4QSam^a variant "fifty," for "ten shekels," and the NJV mentions it in a note. There is a small space in 4QSam^a at this point which is just large enough for exactly four letters to fill in the lacuna. On this basis it is quite likely that the only word that would fit in this space is "fifty," not "ten." This Qumran variant is a good example of evidence based on available space in a defective manuscript, rather than an actual reading, which is, nevertheless, convincing (Ulrich 1978:108).

2 Samuel 19:7 (Hebrew and NJV, v. 8)

The MT has a simple omission, due to haplography, according to Ulrich (1978:86). 4QSam^a, Old Greek, and an ancient Masoretic tradition known as *sebirin,* has a plus, "if you do not come out," which is included in the NJV, NAB, and NRSV.

2 Samuel 21:18-22

The NJV calls attention to the fact that this paragraph also appears in 1 Chronicles 20:4-8. 1QSam (incorrectly cited as 1QSam^a in the NJV note) offers some variants.

2 Samuel 24:20

The NAB includes the 4QSam^a plus, "while he was threshing wheat," found also in 1 Chronicles 21:20 and Josephus' *Antiquities* 7.330 (Loeb). The NJV mentions this reading in a note, while the NRSV does not note it at all. See Ulrich (1978:157-159) for a full analysis of the evidence. Dillard (1985:94-107) discusses how it is possible to decide whether differences between the Samuel and Chronicles parallel accounts are due to textual variants or the hermeneutical perspective. If the former, a case-by-case decision must be made by the translator as to which textual witness is more likely the original. If the latter, the integrity of Samuel and Chronicles should be preserved, rather than harmonized.

2 KINGS

2 Kings 19:25-28

Isaiah's message to King Hezekiah also appears in Isaiah 37. Several textual variants supported by Qumran evidence on Isaiah have been introduced here in the 2 Kings parallel passage by the NEB.

PSALMS

The amount of textual evidence for Psalms that has survived from Qumran is second only to Isaiah. There are at least eighteen copies of Psalms (though most are quite fragmentary) from Cave 4, and at least one copy in each of the other caves that contained biblical manuscripts. Cave 11 yielded the major find, 11QPs[a], as well as other Psalm scroll fragments. This is not surprising, since the book of Psalms was so important in the worship of the community. What did come as a surprise to some was the fact that in a number of the Psalms scrolls, the individual psalms were sometimes in a different order than in our book of Psalms. Some additional psalms were also included. (See part 2 for a discussion of the different ways this evidence has been evaluated.) Sanders's 1967 edition of 11QPs[a] is very helpful in presenting this manuscript. He provides a Hebrew transcription and English translation on facing pages, as well as footnotes indicating where 11QPs[a] differs from the RSV. The individual passages discussed below are those where the translators have relied on Dead Sea Scroll evidence in their work.

Psalm 38:19 (in Hebrew text, 38:20)

The NRSV follows 4QPs[a] in translating "without cause," instead of the MT "living." Other translations, including RSV and NEB/REB, also render "without cause" on the basis of a conjecture inferred from a similar phrase found in Psalm 35:19 and 69:4 (Heb. 5). It is difficult to decide in cases like these whether 4QPs[a] actually read *chnm* "without cause," or whether the scribe was adjusting his text, perhaps unconsciously, to the more familiar phrase. It is certainly possible that an early copy of a text in the Masoretic tradition could have contained a copying error, since there is some similarity between *nun* and *yodh,* especially in the scripts of the Qumran era. In such cases, translators must make a decision and offer the alternate reading in a footnote. It is surprising, however, that REB has not changed the evidence in its note from "conjecture" to "Qumran."

Psalm 69:10 (in Hebrew text, 69:11)

4QPs[a] reads *w'k* instead of the MT *w'bkh* at the beginning of the verse, according to Skehan (1978:175). The NEB, citing Qumran evidence, translates "I have broken," although it is difficult to see how *w'k,* literally "and surely," could yield the NEB text. The REB reverts to translating the MT, "I wept." The RSV and NRSV follow the Old Greek *kai sunekampsa* "I humbled myself." This Qumran reading does not seem to commend itself as a variant to be followed in modern translations, even though the MT is difficult.

Psalm 118:27

The NEB departs from the MT more frequently than any other modern translation. The text of Samuel, with its variants discussed previously, is a special case, because the MT shows many differences from the OG. (The same could be said for Jeremiah, but the fragments found at Qumran are not extensive.)

Psalm 119:37

The NIV translation, "life according to your word," cites as evidence two manuscripts of the Masoretic Text and the Dead Sea Scrolls, in this case 11QPs[a.] While the precise meaning of "two manuscripts of the Masoretic Text" may not be clear to most readers, it does reflect the fact that though there is usually uniformity in the manuscripts of the Masoretic tradition, there are a few textual disagreements among the Masoretic manuscripts. Benjamin Kennicott and J. B. de Rossi, both working in the latter part of the eighteenth century, published extensive examples of these textual variants. Prior to the discovery of the Dead Sea Scrolls, translations would occasionally follow one of these textual variants from these manuscripts, which are generally quite late and which may have introduced a textual variant on the basis of harmonization from parallel passages or the resolution of a textual or grammatical difficulty.

Translations such as the RSV, NEB/REB, and GNB specify that renderings that follow textual variants attested by two or more manuscripts within this Masoretic tradition are not documented by a footnote. In the case of Psalm 119:37, REB translates the minority MT reading *dbrk,* "your word," without any footnote. GNB translates, "as you have promised," a functional equivalent rendering of the same "your word," again without a textual note. The RSV and NJV, on the other hand, translate the majority MT reading, *drkk* "your way." The NIV finds additional support for the MT minority reading in 11QPs[a], and follows that reading in the text. A footnote explains that most of the MT manuscripts read, "your way." There is nothing about the two manuscripts which contain the reading *dbrk* that commends them as having a superior reading. In fact, one of the manuscripts originally had *dbrk,* but the reading was changed. The agreement of 11QPs[a] offers strong support for the antiquity of this reading, but there seems to be no compelling reason to believe that this reading is superior to *drkk.* Both terms are used throughout Psalm 119 as alternate terms for "the Law of the LORD," the Psalm's dominant theme. (See also Psalm 144:2 below.)

Psalm 144:2

As in the case of Psalm 119:37 (discussed above), the NIV recognizes that the MT tradition offers two different readings, with support for the minority reading from 11QPs[a], *'mym* (peoples), instead of the majority reading, *'my* (my people). In addition to the relatively large number of manuscripts that read *'mym,* the MT has a special marginal note called a *sebirin* note. This type of masoretic note offers a suggestion that one might expect *'mym* rather than *'my,* but that is not what is to be read here. A masoretic list cites two other passages, 2 Samuel 22:4 and Lamentations 3:14, where a *sebirin* note appears referring to this same word. The sum of evidence here is weightier than in the case of Psalm 119:37. In fact, the majority of translations render "peoples," but the NIV alone cites the Qumran evidence.

Psalm 145:5

The NIV and REB include the additional phrase found in 11QPs[a], "they will speak." The NJV also cites this evidence in a note. This addition provides a balanced expression for "I will meditate" in the second half of the verse, and it maintains the regular parallelism found throughout most of the Psalm. However, it should also be kept in mind that 1QPs[a] contains a number of textual variants, including a refrain, "Blessed be the LORD and blessed be his name forever and ever" at the end of every verse.

Psalm 145:13

In the MT of this acrostic Psalm there is no line beginning with the letter *nun*. The *nun* line is found in 11QPs[a]. The RSV supplied the *nun* line on the basis of a late Medieval manuscript (Kennicott 145) and the existence of a corresponding line in several ancient versions, including the Old Greek. The NRSV now cites the Qumran evidence. The NEB also included the passage (numbering it a part of 145:14), citing only the Greek evidence. Surprisingly, the REB retains the passage and changes the evidence to Qumran alone. The NIV also includes the lines, also citing Qumran. It should be noted, however, that 11QPs[a] reads "God," instead of "LORD," as in the late Medieval manuscript and the ancient versions.

ISAIAH

The impact of the scrolls of Isaiah on Bible translation has received more attention by far than any of the other biblical books. This is hardly surprising, since 1QIsa[a] was the first Qumran manuscript to be made known to the public, and it remains the best preserved of all the manuscripts, being virtually complete. Morrow (1973) provides a tabulation and description of the textual variants in the rest of the Qumran copies of Isaiah. The decisions of the RSV committee relating to 1QIsa[a] readings are fully described in Burrows (1955:304-313). See also Burrows discussion in *Diligently Compared: The Revised Standard Version and the King James Version of the Old Testament* (1964). Brownlee (1964:216-235) devotes an entire chapter to a discussion of "Superior Readings in the Isaiah Scroll." Peters considers the use of the Isaiah scroll in the RSV and JB (1974). Clark (1984) discusses the influence of the Isaiah scroll on eight modern translations. Clark counts a "total of 113 DSS variant readings [that] have been used in at least one of eight versions studied, though ten of them are used only as marginal alternative readings" (1984:128). Yet only nine variants have been accepted by five or more of these versions; they are 14:4; 21:8; 23:2; 33:8; 49:17, 24; 51:19; 53:11; 60:19 (*ibid.*). In addition to these nine passages, readings of 1QIsa[a] that have been adopted by the NRSV and readings from the other Isaiah manuscripts from Qumran will be considered below.

126

Isaiah 3:24

The RSV and NRSV consider the meaning of the MT difficult and find clarification in 1QIsa[a], which adds *bsht* (shame) following *ky,* understood in its usual meaning of "for" or "because," translating, "for shame shall take the place of beauty." However, HOTTP points out that *ky* can be understood as a noun meaning "branding mark," and the MT can be translated, without resorting to the 1QIsa[a] reading, as does the NJV, "a burn instead of beauty." This would mean that the 1QIsa[a] scribe may have been unfamiliar with the rare meaning of *ky* as a noun and supplied the Hebrew word for "shame" as a reasonable complement.

Isaiah 7:14

NIV, alone, makes note of the 1QIsa[a] reading, *wqr'* (masculine) for the MT *wqr't* (apparently second person feminine singular, but perhaps third person). It seems clear that 1QIsa[a] is once again seeking to simplify a difficult form (Rosenbloom 1970:125). There seems little reason to provide a textual note here.

Isaiah 8:2

The MT and 4QIsa[e] have a first person future verb form for "I will call as witness(es)," while 1QIsa[a] reads *wh'd,* an imperative form, "and have it attested," as in NRSV. The NIV translates the MT (with 4QIsa[e]), "And I will call in Uriah the priest and Zechariah . . . as reliable witnesses for me." Some translations translate the consonants of the MT, but change the vowel of the first letter from w^e to *wa,* changing it to the past tense. The future tense of the NIV, however, is a legitimate tense shift in prophetic literature, reflecting the prophet's certainty that he will be the agent of God's message. In any case, it does not seem necessary to resort to the 1QIsa[a] reading.

Isaiah 11:6

The MT and 4QIsa[c] add to the list of two animals, "calf and beast of prey (lion)," a third, *wmry'* "and the fatling." Early commentators proposed that this noun be emended to a verb, *ymr'w* "will feed." This reading is now found in 1QIsa[a] and is recommended by the HOTTP committee for translation, as in the GNB, "Calves and lion cubs will feed together." The NJV mentions this Qumran reading in a note. The NIV also notes this reading in a footnote but fails to mention the Qumran evidence.

Isaiah 14:4

The NJV, RSV, NRSV, and NIV all follow 1QIsaᵃ in the text. It is the only Qumran reading followed by all eight of the translations studied by Clark (1984). The NJV provides the explanation of this remarkable unanimity: *"madhebah* (the MT) is of unknown meaning." It is likely that one letter, *d,* in the MT is incorrect, and the text should read *r,* a letter that is quite similar in shape. In fact, this is the reading of 1QIsaᵃ: *marhebah,* and is translated "insolence" (NRSV), "fury" (NIV), or in similar terms. In many cases the MT presents difficulties for the translator because of certain obscurities in Hebrew grammar or lexicography. But in some cases, as here, the difficulty is created by textual corruption, and the Qumran evidence provides valuable assistance.

Isaiah 14:30

The RSV and NRSV follow 1QIsaᵃ in translating, "I will slay," instead of "he/it will slay." The Isaiah scroll seems to better fit the context in which this passage is preceded by another first person singular verb. Among the ancient versions, only the Latin agrees with 1QIsaᵃ. Burrows finds the Qumran reading quite convincing (1955:307), and the NEB/REB concur. However, HOTTP prefers the MT, explaining the shift to third person as a reference back to "the venomous serpent" of 14:29.

Isaiah 15:9

In Isaiah's oracle against Moab, the well-known Moabite city of Dibon is mentioned in 15:2. In 15:9 Dimon is mentioned twice in the MT. 1QIsaᵇ agrees with the MT, but is only extant for the first occurrence. The RSV and NRSV follow the 1QIsaᵃ reading, "Dibon," and the NIV cites this Qumran evidence in a note. Should the translator follow 1QIsaᵃ or 1QIsaᵇ? Dimon may be understood as an alternate name for Dibon, using this name as a literary device to sound like the Hebrew word *dam* (blood) in the same verse. This explanation is plausible, since name puns are used elsewhere in the OT. It is also possible that this is another city in Moab, although it is otherwise unknown. The RSV opted for the 1QIsaᵃ harmonization with 15:2. Burrows (1955:307-308) implies that this is one of the thirteen 1QIsaᵃ readings adopted by the RSV committee that he would reject upon later reflection. However, the NRSV retains Dibon. The NEB translates "Dimon," while the

REB renders "Dibon," but fails to offer any textual note, in contradiction to their general policy of citing Qumran evidence.

Isaiah 19:18

In a note, NIV cites Q (= Qumran), along with some MSS of the MT in support of the reading "City of the Sun." Other versions, including RSV and NRSV, read "City of the Sun" in the text without adding a textual note. This follows the general practice of many translations that do not cite textual variants if there is any manuscript support in the Masoretic tradition.

Isaiah 21:8

The NJV offers an English rendering of the difficult MT, "And [like] a lion he called out." The bracketed "like," which is not part of the MT, makes "lion" a simile and helps it to fit the context. Otherwise, "lion" hardly seems appropriate here. Earlier translations resorted to conjectural emendation here, but now 1QIsa^a offers a more intelligible reading, *hr'h* (the lookout/watcher/sentry) for the MT *'ryh* (lion). The NIV, GNB, RSV, and NRSV all follow the Qumran reading in the text. HOTTP suggests that translators may follow 1QIsa^a, although it believes that this is "certainly not the original text."

Isaiah 23:2-3

1QIsa^a differs from the last word of verse 2 in two letters, adding *kaph* and reading *yodh* instead of *waw*, "your messengers," instead of "they filled you." 1QIsa^b appears to offer the same reading, although 4QIsa^a reads *ml'k,* probably in agreement with the MT. The NAB, RSV, and NRSV follow Qumran, connecting "messengers" with the "merchants" of the previous line. The NJV and NIV translate the MT, and NIV gives the Qumran reading in a note. It is reasonable to assume that 1QIsa^a preserves the better reading here.

Isaiah 29:5

The RSV translates the first line of the verse, "But the multitude of your foes," adding a footnote to explain that "foes" is based on a conjecture for the MT *zryk* (your strangers). The NRSV has made no change here, but the NAB follows 1QIsa^a *zdyk* "your arrogance," and the NJV cites the same Qumran evidence in a footnote. Apparently, the NRSV did not find the Qumran evidence compelling and retained the conjecture to clarify the more difficult reading of the MT. The GNB translates it "foreigners," a rendering that is appropriate to the context.

Isaiah 33:8

The RSV, NRSV, NAB, and NIV follow 1QIsa[a] in reading *'dym* "witnesses" instead of the MT *'rym* "cities." "Witnesses" seems appropriate to the meaning of the passage, and the interchange of *resh* for *daleth* is understandable in light of the similarity of the letter shapes. The NJV also calls attention to this reading in a footnote.

Isaiah 34:5

The NJV cites the 1QIsa[a] variant, "be seen," in a note. The NEB and REB place the Qumran reading, *tr'h,* in the text. Other modern translations follow the MT, "be drunk," although the GNB, "The LORD has prepared his sword in heaven" may be based on a conjecture that adds *mem* to the beginning of the word.

Isaiah 37:25

Although the NIV generally follows the MT more often than other modern translations, in this case the NIV alone puts the reading of 1QIsa[a], *zrym* (foreign), in its translation, "I have dug wells in foreign lands and drunk the water there." While this is a plausible reading, it may be a case of assimilation to a parallel passage in 2 Kings 19:24. 1QIsa[a] contains a number of other examples of assimilation to parallel passages in Kings.

Isaiah 37:27

The RSV and NRSV translators were influenced in their translation here by the parallel passage of 2 Kings 19:26, preferring "blighted" for the MT "field." The NJV and NIV cite 1QIsa[a]'s reading, *hnshdp,* and translate "blasted/scorched," which appears to be the preferred reading.

Isaiah 45:2

The second line in the MT reads, "I will level the swellings/rough places." The Hebrew word rendered "swellings" occurs only here in the OT. 1QIsa[a] reads *hrrym* "mountains," which is followed by the NIV, NAB, and RSV/NRSV.

130

Isaiah 45:8

The RSV and NRSV follow the 1QIsa[a] reading *wyprch* for the MT *wyprw,* a difference of only one letter, *cheth* for *waw,* which yields the translation, "that salvation may sprout forth [RSV]/spring up [NRSV]," instead of, "that they may bring forth salvation." The NAB follows the same Qumran reading. The NEB and GNB, in dynamic equivalent renderings, demonstrate that both the MT and Qumran express a common idea. The NEB translates, "that it may bear the fruit of salvation," and the GNB has, "[it] will blossom with freedom and justice." Neither translation has a textual note here. HOTTP prefers the Qumran reading, but as can be seen, there may be little difference in the translation of the MT or Qumran.

Isaiah 49:12

The MT says that the people of "Sinim" will come to Zion, but this place name is otherwise unknown. 1QIsa[a] gives the name as "Syene" which is located in Egypt and is known today as Aswan. This was the location of a Jewish settlement known as Elephantine. The NAB, NIV, and RSV/NRSV all follow the Qumran reading here. The NEB also translates "Syene," identifying this as a scroll reading. The REB retains "Syene," but has dropped the footnote. This is either an oversight or an exegetical decision on the part of the translators to identify the MT "Sinim" as "Syene/Aswan," without resorting to a textual variant. The NJV cites the variant in a footnote.

Isaiah 49:24

The phrase "captives of the just" in the second half of 49:24 is somewhat awkward in this context. The NIV, RSV/NRSV, NEB/REB, and NAB all follow the 1QIsa[a] reading, *'ryts* (tyrant/ruthless), citing the manuscript evidence from Qumran. GNB also translates "tyrant" without a textual note, since GNB does not cite textual variants that have the support of at least one Hebrew manuscript. HOTTP recommends that translations follow the Qumran reading.

Isaiah 51:19

This verse ends in the MT with the question, "How can I comfort you?" In 1QIsa[a] the word for "comfort" begins with the letter *yod* instead of *aleph* (third person instead of first). The NAB, NIV, RSV/NRSV, and NEB/REB all follow the Qumran reading, although HOTTP believes the MT should be followed in translation and considers the 1QIsa^a reading an assimilation to the third person verb used earlier in the verse. There is no compelling reason to doubt that in the prophetic style, God would be speaking in the second half of the verse. The acceptance by most modern translations of this Qumran variant illustrates how an evaluation of manuscript evidence can be combined with a decision regarding literary appropriateness. This has been the traditional approach of translators when dealing with textual problems. A newer trend, as exemplified by HOTTP, tends to evaluate variants such as found in 1QIsa^a here, as just as likely to be the result of an ancient scribe adjusting the text in response to some perceived difficulty. Accordingly, modern translators would be advised to be a bit more cautious in accepting textual variants of this type.

Isaiah 53:11

Many recent translations, including the NIV, NAB, NEB/REB, and NRSV, accept the addition of the word *'wr* "light," in both 1QIsa^a and 1QIsa^b. Not only is the weight of the manuscript convincing to these translators, but the balance of the parallelism is improved as well. HOTTP agrees that translators should follow the Qumran reading here. Morrow (1973:143), however, disagrees, calling attention to the fact that "light" plays a significant role in the theology of the Qumran community. The assumption that the Qumran scribes would have added "light" to the text presupposes that both copies were made at Qumran, which is not necessarily the case.

Isaiah 60:19

The NJV and RSV/NRSV follow the addition of *blylh* "in the night" in 1QIsa^a. As in several other cases such as 53:11, this Qumran addition gives the parallelism of the verse better balance. However, one must be cautious about accepting readings that could have been motivated by the scribe's sensitivity to Hebrew poetic style. This is why HOTTP does not advise translators to follow 1QIsa^a here, even though many modern translations do.

JEREMIAH

It seems surprising that there are only three citations of Qumran evidence in Jeremiah, which is one of the longest books of the OT and a book that differs significantly both in length and chapter arrangement between the MT and the OG versions. In fact, two of the three textual notes cite an uncertain source, reducing the number of verifiable variants considered in major translations to one! Whether an accident of history, or lesser Qumran interest in the book than Isaiah, there were only a few copies of Jeremiah found at Qumran, one in Cave 2 and, by initial count, three in Cave 4—although Tov (1989) now believes that the original 4QJer[b] actually consists of three different manuscripts (see part 2, p. 72). Because of the relative paucity of material, it is likely that there will be few additional specific Qumran passages cited in translations and revisions of the future. However, the existence at Qumran of Hebrew manuscripts that correspond both to the longer MT text and the shorter OG text demonstrate that both editions were known at a relatively early stage of the transmission of the text.

Jeremiah 3:1
The Old Greek text omits the word "saying" at the beginning of this verse. It seems to be an unnecessary introduction to chapter 3, since both chapters 2 and 3:1-5 are "the word of the LORD." The RSV omitted "saying" on the authority of the Greek evidence, as do the NAB, NEB/REB, and GNB (without any textual note). The NRSV omits "saying" and cites Qumran evidence; in 3:8 another Qumran variant is reported and followed, rendering "She saw," instead of "I saw" of the MT. In both cases, however, no Qumran manuscript is known to contain chapter 3 (Tov 1989:189-206).

Jeremiah 47:5
In a footnote NEB cites the reading of 2QJer "roll about," instead of the MT "gash yourselves." The REB retains "gash yourselves" in the text and omits the textual note on the Qumran evidence. Other recent translations have not considered this Qumran variant, either.

DANIEL
The ancient Greek translation of almost the entire Old Testament derives from a version commonly known as the Septuagint and is found in the great Uncial manuscripts, Sinaiticus, Alexandrinus, and Vaticanus. The book of Daniel is a unique exception. The Greek version of Daniel found

in these manuscripts and most printed editions of the Septuagint is derived from a work by Theodotion. His translation of Daniel supplanted the traditional Old Greek version to such an extent that only one manuscript of the Old Greek version remains in existence today. The rest of his translation work was not nearly so successful, although the influence of his work can be seen in the revision of Exodus and Job, as well as in the work of Origen. Actually, little is known about the man Theodotion. Although he probably lived in the second century A.D., there is early evidence of Greek translation and revision along the lines followed by Theodotion. This translation activity is sometimes ascribed to proto-Theodotion or Ur-Theodotion. Some of the readings in the Daniel manuscripts from Qumran appear to be an original Hebrew version of the proto-Theodotion translation.

Daniel 7:1-2

The RSV ends 7:1 with the phrase found in the MT, "and [Daniel] told the sum of the matter." Theodotion's Greek version omits the Aramaic word *'mr* (say), but the RSV did not follow this reading on the strength of this Greek witness alone. The NRSV, however, noting that 4QDan[b] also omits *'mr,* adopts this reading for the text and relegates "he said" to the footnote.

Daniel 8:2

The clause "I saw in the vision" is repeated in 8:2. The second occurrence appears to be unnecessary, creating a rather cumbersome sentence. In fact, Theodotion has the clause only once. As in the case of Daniel 7:1, the RSV does not depart from the MT. The NRSV finds support for the Theodotionic reading from Qumran evidence, although Ulrich (1987:34; 1989:16) does not offer this omission as a variant in either 4QDan[a] or 4QDan[b], the only two Qumran manuscripts that contain this verse. In 4QDan[a] *bchzwn* "in the vision" clearly occurs twice. 1QDan[b] is more fragmentary; but *bchzwn* occurs in the second half of the verse, while the first words of the verse are missing in the fragment. The only possibility, although a remote one (based on conjectured line length), is the omission of the first occurrence; but it is the second occurrence that is omitted by the ancient Greek witnesses.

MINOR PROPHETS

Among the documents found at Qumran are fifteen manuscripts that are commentaries on biblical texts (technically called *pesharim*). There are commentaries on Psalms (3 copies), Isaiah (5), Hosea (2), Micah (1), Nahum (1), Zephaniah (2), and Habakkuk (1). There are small fragments of four additional manuscripts which some have classified as *pesharim,* but evidence is insufficient or completely lacking to prove that they belong in this category of literature. The most famous *pesher,* found with the first group of scrolls brought to light from Cave 1, is 1QpHab. The Cave 4 *pesharim* were published by Allegro in DJD 5, although the accuracy of his work has been criticized by many scholars. All the *pesharim* have been collected in a single volume, complete with transcription of the Hebrew text, English translation, and extensive notes by Horgan (1979). This remains the most convenient resource for studying the *pesharim* Qumran manuscripts.

The general format of the *pesharim* commentaries is a citation of the biblical text, generally followed by *pishro* "its interpretation," or a similar phrase. The Hebrew word *pesher* occurs only once in the Hebrew Bible in Ecclesiastes 8:1, "Who knows the interpetation of a thing?" (RSV). The interpretations offered in the Qumran *pesharim* generally deal with the application of the biblical text to the contemporary situation. The *pesharim* provide many insights into a type of biblical exegesis practiced in the years surrounding the life of Jesus. The perspective on historical and current events in the life of the community also gives us a perspective on their theological outlook on history.

For the purposes of our study of the use of the actual biblical quotations found in the *pesharim,* several factors must be kept in mind. First, minor adjustments of the biblical text often occured so as to adjust it to the syntax of the larger context. Of even greater importance in the evaluation of the value of the *pesharim* for textual criticism is the realization that "where one [textual] reading suits the commentator's purpose better than another, he will use it, although he may show in the course of his comment that he is aware of an alternative reading. He has been suspected of deliberately altering the text here and there in order to make the application more pointed, but the suspicion does not amount to proof" (Bruce 1959:12). With these cautions in mind, we can turn to the specific passages where translators have utilized the evidence of the *pesharim.*

Nahum 3:8

In 1QpNah a feminine pronoun suffix, -h, is added to the word *chel* (rampart). The NEB calls attention to this reading in 1QpNah. The REB has not revised the translation, "whose rampart was the Nile," but has dropped the footnote. In fact, most translations render this passage similarly, adding the pronoun which is appropriate to good English style. They were preceded by the ancient versions in making a syntactic adjustment. The question remains whether the 1QpNah scribe was faithfully reproducing a Hebrew text that included the suffix -h, or whether he, too, was improving the smoothness of the sentence.

Habakkuk 1:8

The MT repeats the Hebrew noun with a pronoun suffix, *parashayw uparashayw* "their horsemen, yea their horsemen" (RSV). 1QpHab omits one letter, *yodh,* in the second occurrence, making it a plural verb. The NEB follows this reading and translates, "their cavalry [i.e., horsemen] spring forward, they spring forward." The REB, following the same textual variant, renders it more smoothly, "their cavalry prance and [they] gallop." Other translations follow the MT here.

Habakkuk 1:17

In 1QpHab the Hebrew word *chrm* (dragnet) in the MT differs by one letter, *chrb* (sword). In the MT the "dragnet" metaphor is repeated from verse 16 but seems somewhat out of place in this verse. The 1QpHab figure of the sword fits the context of the entire verse, "keep on unsheathing his sword (instead of "keep on emptying his net") and continually slay nations without pity." The NEB/REB follows the 1QpHab reading, as does the NAB, but without noting such in the collection of "Textual Notes." The GNB also follows 1QpHab without a textual note, but this is consistent with their general policy of not footnoting a textual variant that is found in at least one Hebrew manuscript. The NRSV retains the MT without any note; the NJV offers the 1QpHab reading in a note. The consensus of modern exegetes and translators is in favor of the 1QpHab as superior. HOTTP supports this decision as well.

Habakkuk 2:1

The NJV offers the 1QpHab reading "at my post" for the MT "at the post" in a footnote. The only difference between the MT *mtswr* and 1QpHab *mtswry* is the addition of the pronoun suffix *-y*. This variant is of relatively minor importance, and most translations simply follow the MT here. However, in the same verse, there is a question as to the sequence of dialogue between the prophet and God. Habakkuk has made his complaint and waits at his post for the Lord's reply. The question is whether the last clause of the sentence is a parallel statement ("the LORD will say" parallel to the expression "he will answer") or the next stage in the dialogue, "I [Habakkuk] will answer." Unfortunately, the 1QpHab manuscript is missing here. The ancient Syriac translation has "he will answer," and this variant is followed by the NRSV (but not RSV), NAB, and GNB.

Habakkuk 2:5

The Lord responds to Habakkuk's complaint: "the sins of the wicked will not go unpunished." A variety of terms are used throughout chapter 2 to describe the wicked. In the MT 2:5 says, "wine is treacherous (Hebrew, *hayyayin*). Although drinking is condemned in 2:15, here in 2:5, reference to a person seems more appropriate. 1QpHab reads *hwn* instead of the MT *hayyayin,* which can be interpreted as *hwn,* "wealth(y)" (NRSV, GNB) or as *hawwan* "defiant/conceited" (NJV/REB). The latter interpretation is supported by some ancient Greek manuscripts. In this passage the more difficult reading *hawwan* seems best to explain how the other, easier readings could have arisen.

Habakkuk 2:15-16

In the last word of verse 15, 1QpHab differs from the MT by one letter: *daleth* instead of *resh* changes the MT *me'orehem* "their nakedness" to *mw'dyhm* "their appointed feasts." Only the NEB/REB calls attention to this Qumran variant in a note, while translating the MT in the text. However, another variant of 1QpHab in verse 16 has been widely accepted by translators. This variant involves the transposition of two consonants: the MT *wh'rl* — 1QpHab *whr'l.* The meaning of the MT is obscure, although it probably means "be exposed" (NIV) or "be uncircumcised" (RSV), while *hr'l* in 1QpHab means "stagger." However, although the quotation of the biblical text by the commentator of 1QpHab reads "stagger," his *pesher* comments seem to build on the reading found in the MT, because he says that the shame of the Wicked Priest was greater than his glory

137

"because he did not circumcise the foreskin of his heart but walked in the ways of drunkenness." The NEB/REB, GNB, NRSV, and NAB all follow the text of 1QpHab. The RSV also translates "stagger," but bases this rendering on a conjecture.

Conclusion

Our survey of the Dead Sea Scroll biblical manuscripts and their impact on recent Bible translations is more of a preface than a conclusion. It has taken over forty years for the raw data of the biblical manuscripts from the Dead Sea region study to become available. Because of the fragmentary nature of many of the manuscripts, studies have taken longer than what was first promised. The accumulated evidence of the study of the manuscripts is only now reshaping our understanding of the history of the Old Testament text around the turn of the era.

Over thirty-five years ago Dewey M. Beegle (1957) assessed the impact of the Dead Sea Scroll discoveries on Old Testament translation by observing that, even though the manuscript evidence was incomplete, several tentative conclusions could be reached (1957). Now that nearly all of the biblical manuscripts from Qumran are accessible, the complete picture confirms Beegle's conclusions: (1) The scrolls confirm the reliability of the Masoretic Text, thereby adding almost a thousand years to the antiquity of the Hebrew text. (2) They reestablish the Septuagint as a textual authority. (3) The scrolls are a source of reliable variant readings.

The enthusiasm created by the initial discoveries prompted Bible translators to consider changes in the Old Testament text based on the Dead Sea Scrolls. The Revised Standard Version was the first translation to utilize the Qumran evidence. Since then, every major translation has taken into account the evidence of the Dead Sea Scrolls, some offering only occasional notes and others utilizing the evidence quite extensively. All future translations will be able to take advantage of the full range of evidence now available and will be able to give consideration to the textual history of the Old Testament as it is being rewritten by the Qumran finds. Those who anticipated some revolutionary revelations which would require dramatic changes in the Old Testament will be disappointed. The textual evidence of the Dead Sea Scrolls, in fact, confirms the general reliability and stability of the text of the Old Testament as we have it today, while at the same time offers evidence of important early witnesses to textual variants. Even the nonbiblical manuscript evidence will play an indirect role in the work of the translators by providing a detailed picture of one Jewish group of the first century, their theology, and their method of biblical interpretation. The next chapter in the history of Bible translation is about to be written.

Biblical Passages in the Old Testament Manuscripts:
A Listing from Genesis to Malachi

Manuscripts whose contents are not yet known are listed in parentheses at the end of the entries for some individual books. If a manuscript has not received full official publication, but some information is known about its content, this fact is indicated in the index. If parts of a chapter are known to be present in the manuscript, but no additional information is available, the chapter number is followed by ♦. If more information is known about the content but not the exact extent of the material included, the index entry will indicate this uncertainty with a question mark, as follows: (?). Until these manuscripts are fully published, one cannot be entirely certain that a verse at the end of one or the beginning of the next chapter is included in the fragment. The symbol (!) after certain portions indicates that the verses so designated are transposed in the manuscript.

GENESIS

1:1-11, 13-22	4QGen g
1:1-27	4QGen b
1:8-10	4QGen h(1)
1:9, 14-16, 27-26(!)	4QGen k
1:18-21	1QGen
1:18-27	4QGen d
2:1-3	4QGen k
2:6-7 or 18-19	4QGen g
2:14-19	4QGen b
2:17-18	4QGen h(2)
3:1-2	4QGen k
3:11-14	1QGen
4:2-11	4QGen b
5:13 or 14	4QGen b
6:13-21	6QpaleoGen
12:4-5	4QGen h(par)
17:12-19	8QGen
18:20-25	8QGen
19:27-28	2QGen

22:13-15	1QGen
22 ♦	4QGen(+Exod) a
23:17-19	1QGen
24:22-24	1QGen
26:21-26	4QpaleoGen l
27 ♦	4QGen(+Exod) a
32:4-5, 30, 33(?)	(2)MurGen
33:1	(2)MurGen
33:18-20(?)	Mur(?)Gen
34:1(?)-3	Mur(?)Gen
34:5-7, 30-31(?)	(2)MurGen
34 ♦	4QGen(+Exod) a
35:1, 4-7	(2)MurGen
35:6-10	Hev(?)Gen
35 ♦	4QGen(+Exod) a
36:5-12	Hev(?)Gen
36:6, 35-37	2QGen
36 ♦	4QGen(+Exod) a
36 ♦	4QGen e
37 ♦	4QGen(+Exod) a
37 ♦	4QGen e
39 ♦	4QGen(+Exod) a
40:23	4QGen c
40 ♦	4QGen(+Exod) a
40 ♦	4QGen e
41:1-11	4QGen c
41 ♦	4QGen e
41 ♦	4QGen j
42 ♦	4QGen e
42 ♦	4QGen j
43 ♦	4QGen e
43 ♦	4QGen j
45 ♦	4QGen(+Exod) a
45 ♦	4QGen j
46:7-11	MasGen
46 ♦	4QGen(+Exod) a
47 ♦	4QGen(+Exod) a
48:1-11	4QGen f
48 ♦	4QGen(+Exod) a
49 ♦	4QGen(+Exod) a
49 ♦	4QGen e
50:26(?)	4QpaleoGen (+Exod) l

EXODUS

1:1-5	4QExod b
1:1-5	4Qpaleo(Gen+)Exod l

Biblical Passages in the Old Testament Manuscripts:
A Listing from Genesis to Malachi

Manuscripts whose contents are not yet known are listed in parentheses at the end of the entries for some individual books. If a manuscript has not received full official publication, but some information is known about its content, this fact is indicated in the index. If parts of a chapter are known to be present in the manuscript, but no additional information is available, the chapter number is followed by ♦. If more information is known about the content but not the exact extent of the material included, the index entry will indicate this uncertainty with a question mark, as follows: (?). Until these manuscripts are fully published, one cannot be entirely certain that a verse at the end of one or the beginning of the next chapter is included in the fragment. The symbol (!) after certain portions indicates that the verses so designated are transposed in the manuscript.

GENESIS

1:1-11, 13-22	4QGen g
1:1-27	4QGen b
1:8-10	4QGen h(1)
1:9, 14-16, 27-26(!)	4QGen k
1:18-21	1QGen
1:18-27	4QGen d
2:1-3	4QGen k
2:6-7 or 18-19	4QGen g
2:14-19	4QGen b
2:17-18	4QGen h(2)
3:1-2	4QGen k
3:11-14	1QGen
4:2-11	4QGen b
5:13 or 14	4QGen b
6:13-21	6QpaleoGen
12:4-5	4QGen h(par)
17:12-19	8QGen
18:20-25	8QGen
19:27-28	2QGen

EXODUS

18:1-27	4QpaleoExod m
18:17-24	4Qpaleo(Gen+)Exod l
18:21-22	2QExod b
19:1, 7-17, 23-25	4QpaleoExod m
19:9	2QExod b
19:24-25	1QExod
19:24-25	4Qpaleo(Gen+)Exod l
20:1, 18-19	4QpaleoExod m
20:1, 25-26	1QExod
20:1-2	4Qpaleo(Gen+)Exod l
21:1, 4-5	1QExod
21:5-6, 13-14, 22-32	4QpaleoExod m
21:18-20(?)	2QExod a
21:37	2QExod b
22:1-2, 15-19	2QExod b
22:3-4, 6-7, 11-13, 16-19, 20-30	4QpaleoExod m
22:23-24	4Qpaleo(Gen+)Exod l
23:5-16	4Qpaleo(Gen+)Exod l
23:15-16, 19-31	4QpaleoExod m
24:1-4, 6-11	4QpaleoExod m
25:7-20	4Qpaleo(Gen+)Exod l
25:11-12, 20-29, 31-34	4QpaleoExod m
26:8-9	4QExod k
26:8-15, 21-30	4QpaleoExod m
26:11-13	2QExod a
26:29-37	4Qpaleo(Gen+)Exod l
27:1, 6-14	4Qpaleo(Gen+)Exod l
27:1-3, 9-14, 18-19	4QpaleoExod m
27:17-19	2QExod b
28:3-4, 8-12, 22-24, 26-28, 30-43	4QpaleoExod m
28:4-7	7QExodpapGk
28:33-35, 40-42	4Qpaleo(Gen+)Exod l
29:1-5, 20, 22-25, 31-41	4QpaleoExod m
30:10 [after chap. 26], 12-18, 29-31, 34-38	4QpaleoExod m
30:21(?), 23-25	2QExod a
31:1-8, 13-15	4QpaleoExod m
31:16-17	2QExod b
32:2-19, 25-30	4QoaleoExod m
32:32-34	2QExod a
33:12-23	4QpaleoExod m
34:1-3, 10-13, 15-18, 20-24, 27-28	4QpaleoExod m
34:10	2QExod b
35:1	4QpaleoExod m
36:21-24	4QpaloeExod m
36:34-36	4Qpaleo(Gen+)Exod l
36 ♦	4QpaleoExod m

Manuscript known to exist but contents not yet published:
4QExod j

LEVITICUS

20:20-24 . . . . 1QpaleoLev(+Num)
21:6-11 . . . . 11QpaleoLev
21:24(?) . . . . 1QpaleoLev(+Num)
22:2-6 . . . . 1QpaleoLev(+Num)
22:9-33 . . . . 4QLev b
22:21-27 . . . . 11QpaleoLev
23:2-8, 11-14, 16-22 . . . . 4QLev b
23:4-8 . . . . 1QpaleoLev(+Num)
23:22-29 . . . . 11QpaleoLev
24:3-23 . . . . 4QLev b
24:9-14 . . . . 11QpaleoLev
25:28-29, 45-49 . . . . 4QLev b
25:28-36 . . . . 11QpaleoLev
26:2-16 . . . . 4QgkLev a
26:17-26 . . . . 11QpaleoLev
27:10-12 . . . . 4QLev(+Num) a
27:11-19 . . . . 11QpaleoLev

NUMBERS

1:36-40 . . . . 4Q(Lev+)Num a
1:48-50 . . . . 1Qpaleo(Lev+)Num
2:31-32 . . . . 4Q(Lev+)Num a
3:5-8, 10-18 . . . . 4Q(Lev+)Num a
3:38-41, 51 . . . . 2QNum a
3:40-42 . . . . 4QgkNum
4:1-3 . . . . 2QNum a
4:2-3, 5-11, 40-44, 47 . . . . 4Q(Lev+)Num a
4:6-9, 11-14 . . . . 4QgkNum
7:88 . . . . 2QNum c
8:7-12 . . . . 4Q(Lev+)Num a
9:3-10, 19-20 . . . . 4Q(Lev+)Num a
11:31-35 . . . . 4QNum b
12:1(?)-6, 8-11 . . . . 4QNum b
12:4-11 . . . . 4Q(Lev+)Num a
13:7, 10-13, 15-24 . . . . 4QNum b
13:18 . . . . 4Q(Lev+)Num a
15:41 . . . . 4QNum b
16:1(?)-11 . . . . 4QNum b
17:12-17 . . . . 4QNum b
18:8-9 . . . . 2QNum d?
18:25-32 . . . . 4QNum b
19:1(?)-6 . . . . 4QNum b
20:7-8 . . . . 5/6 HevNum
20:12-13b [= Sam add], 16-17, 19-29(?) . . . . . 4QNum b
21:1(?)-2, 12a-13a [= Sam add], 20-21a (Sam) . . 4QNum b
22:5-21, 31-34, 37-38, 41(?) . . . . 4QNum b

DEUTERONOMY

7:19-22 . . . . 4QDeut m
7:21-26 . . . . 4QDeut f
8:1-5 . . . . 4QDeut c
8:1-16 . . . . 4QDeut e
8:2-14 . . . . 4QDeut f
8:5-10 . . . . 4QDeut j
8:5-10 . . . . 4QDeut n
8:5-20 . . . . 5QDeut
8:8-9 . . . . 1QDeut b
8:18-19 . . . . 1QDeut a
9:1-2 . . . . 5QDeut
9:6-7 . . . . 4QDeut f
9:10 . . . . 1QDeut b
9:11-12, 17-19, 29 . . . . 4QDeut c
9:12-14 . . . . 4QDeut g
9:27-28 . . . . 1QDeut a
10:1-2, 5-8 . . . . 4QDeut c
10:1-3 . . . . (1)MurDeut
10:8-12 . . . . 2QDeut c
10:12, 14 . . . . 4QDeut l
11:2-3 . . . . (1)MurDeut
11:2-4, 9-13, 18-19 . . . . 4QDeut c
11:4 . . . . 4QgkDeut
11:6-10, 12-13 . . . . 4QDeut j
11:6-13 . . . . 4QDeut k1
11:27-30 . . . . 1QDeut a
11:28, 30-32 . . . . 4QpaleoDeut r
11:30-31 . . . . 1QDeut b
12:1-5, 11-12, 22 . . . . 4QpaleoDeut r
12:18-19, 26, 30-31 . . . . 4QDeut c
12:25-26 . . . . (1)MurDeut
12:43-51 . . . . 4QDeut j
13:1-5 . . . . 4QDeut j
13:1-6, 13-14 . . . . 1QDeut a
13:5-7, 11-12, 16 . . . . 4QDeut c
13:19 . . . . 4QpaleoDeut r
14:1-4, 19-22, 26-29 . . . . 4QpaleoDeut r
14:21, 24-25 . . . . 1QDeut a
14:29(?) . . . . (1)MurDeut
15:1 (or 2) . . . . (1)MurDeut
15:1-5, 15-19 . . . . 4QDeut c
15:5-6, 8-10 . . . . 4QpaleoDeut r
15:14-15 . . . . 1QDeut b
16:2-3, 5-11, 20-22(?) . . . . 4QDeut c
16:4, 6-7 . . . . 1QDeut a
17:1(?)-7, 15-20(?) . . . . 4QDeut c
17:12-15 . . . . 2QDeut b

29:9-20 . . . . 1QDeut b
29:17-19 . . . . 4QDeut c
29:22-25 . . . . 4QDeut o
29:24-27 . . . . 4QDeut b
30:3-14 . . . . 4QDeut b
30:19-20 . . . . 1QDeut b
31:1-10, 12-13 . . . . 1QDeut b
31:9-10 . . . . 4QDeut h
31:9-14, 15-17, 24-30(?) . . . . 4QDeut b
31:12 . . . . 4QDeut l
31:16-19 . . . . 4QDeut c
31:29 . . . . 4QpaleoDeut r
32:1-3 . . . . 4QDeut b
32:6-8, 10-11, 13-14, 33-35 . . . . 4QpaleoDeut r
32:7-8 . . . . 4QDeut j
32:17-18, 22-23, 25-27 . . . . 4QDeut k1
32:17-29 +16-19 . . . . 1QDeut b
32:37-43 . . . . 4QDeut q
33:1-2 . . . . 4QDeut l
33:2-8, 29 . . . . 4QpaleoDeut r
33:3 . . . . 4QDeut c
33:9-11 . . . . 4QDeut h
33:12-24 . . . . 1QDeut b
33 ◆ . . . . MasDeut
34:1 . . . . 4QpaleoDeut r
34:4-6, 8 . . . . 4QDeut l
34 ◆ . . . . MasDeut

JOSHUA

2:11-12 . . . . 4QJosh b
2 ◆ . . . . 4QJosh a
3:15-17 . . . . 4QJosh b
3 ◆ . . . . 4QJosh a
4:1-3 . . . . 4QJosh b
4 ◆ . . . . 4QJosh a
5 ◆ . . . . 4QJosh a
6:5-10 . . . . 4QJosh a
7:12-15 [Reed -16] . . . . 4QJosh a
8:3-19, 34-35 . . . . 4QJosh a
10:3-11 . . . . 4QJosh a
17:11-15 . . . . 4QJosh b

JUDGES

6:2-6, 11-13 . . . . 4QJudg a
6:20-22 . . . . 1QJudg

2 SAMUEL

2:5-16, 25-27, 29-32	. . 4QSam a
3:1-8, 23-39	. . 4QSam a
4:1-4, 9-12	. . 4QSam a
5:1-16 (omit 4-5)	. . 4QSam a
6:2-9, 12-18	. . 4QSam a
7:23-29	. . 4QSam a
8:2-8	. . 4QSam a
10:4-7, 18-19	. . 4QSam a
11:2-12, 16-20	. . 4QSam a
12:4-5, 8-9, 13-20, 30-31	. . 4QSam a
13:1-6, 13-34, 36-39	. . 4QSam a
14:1-3, 18-19	. . 4QSam a
14:7-33	. . 4QSam c
15:1-6, 27-31	. . 4QSam a
15:1-15	. . 4QSam c
16:1-2, 11-13, 17-18, 21-23	. . 4QSam a
18:2-7, 9-11	. . 4QSam a
19:7-12	. . 4QSam a
20:2-3, 9-14, 23-26	. . 4QSam a
20:6-10	. . 1QSam
21:1-2, 4-6, 15-17	. . 4QSam a
21:16-18	. . 1QSam
22:30-51	. . 4QSam a
23:1-6	. . 4QSam a
23:7	. . 11QPs a
23:9-12	. . 1QSam
24:16-20	. . 4QSam a

1 KINGS

1:1, 16-17, 27-37	. . 5QKgs
3:12-14	. . 6QpapKgs
7:31-41	. . 4QKgs
8:1-9, 16-18	. . 4QKgs
12:28-31	. . 6QpapKgs
22:28-31	. . 6QpapKgs

2 KINGS

5:26	. . 6QpapKgs
6:32	. . 6QpapKgs
7:8-10, 20	. . 6QpapKgs
8:1-5	. . 6QpapKgs
9:1-2	. . 6QpapKgs
10:19-21	. . 6QpapKgs

PSALMS

Passage	Scroll
2:1-8	11QPs c
2:6-7	3QPs
5:8-13	4QPs s
5:9-13	4QPs a
6:1	4QPs s
6:1-4	4QPs a
9:3-7	11QPs c
12:5-9	11QPs c
13:1-6	11QPs c
14:1-6	11QPs c
15:1-5	5/6HevPs
16:1	5/6HevPs
16:7-9	4QPs c
17:5-9, 14	8QPs
17:9-15	11QPs c
18:1-12	11QPs c
18:3-14, 16-18, 33-41	4QPs c
18:6-9, 10-13	8QPs
22:14-17	4QPs f
25:15	4QPs a
26:7-12	4QPs r
27:1	4QPs r
27:12-14	4QPs c
28:1-2, 4	4QPs c
30:9-13	4QPs r
31:24-25(?)	4QPs a
31:25	4QPs q
33:1-12	4QPs a
33:1-18	4QPs q
35:2, 14-20, 26-28	4QPs a
35:4-20	4QPs q
35:15-28	11QPs cS
35:27-28	4QPs c
36:1-9	4QPs a
36:1-13	11QPs cS
37:1-40	11QPs cS
37:18-19	4QPs c
38:1-23	11QPs cS
38:2-12, 16-23	4QPs a
39:1-14	11QPs cS
39:13-14	11QPs d
40:1	11QPs d
42:5	4QPs frg1
43:1-3	11QPs d
44:3-5, 7, 9, 23-25	1QPs c

94:1-4, 8-14, 17-18, 21-22	4QPs b
94:16	1QPs a
95:3-6	4QPs m
95:11	1QPs a
96:2	1QPs a
96:2	4QPs b
97:6-9	4QPs m
98:4	4QPs b
98:4-8	4QPs m
99:1	4QPs frg3
99:5-6	4QPs b
100:1-2	4QPs b
101:1-8	11QPs a
102:1-2, 18-29	11QPs a
102:5(?), 10-29	4QPs b
103:1	11QPs a
103:1-6, 9-14, 20-21	4QPs b
103:2-11	2QPs
104:1-3, 20, 21	4QPs e
104:1-5, 8-11, 14-15, 22-25, 33-35	4QPs d
104:1-6, 21-35	11QPs a
104:3-5, 11-12	4QPs l
104:6-11	2QPs
105:1-12, 25-45	11QPs a
105:22-24, 36-45	4QPs e
107:2-4, 8-11, 13-15, 18-19, 22-30, 35-42	4QPs f
109:4-6, 25-28	4QPs f
109:13	4QPs e
109:21-31	11QPs a
112:4-5	4QPs b
113:1	4QPs b
114:7-8	4QPs o
115:1-4	4QPs o
115:2-3	4QPs b
115:15-18	4QPs e
116:1-3	4QPs e
116:5-10	4QPs o
116:17-19	4QPs b
118:1-3, 6-11, 18-20, 23-26, 29	4QPs b
118:1, 15, 16, 8, 9, 29(!)	11QPs a
118:1(?), 15-16	11QPs b
118:25-29	11QPs a
119:1-6, 15-25, 37-49, 59-73, 82-96, 105-112	11QPs a
119:10-21	4QPs h
119:31-34, 43-48, 77-79	1QPs a
119:37-43, 44-46, 49-50, 73, 81-83, 90-92	4QPs g
119:99-101, 104, 113-120, 138-142	5QPs

150:1-6 . . . . MasPs b
151 (or 151A) . . . . 11QPs a
152 (or 151B) . . . . 11QPs a
154:3-19 . . . . 11QPs a
155:1-19 . . . . 11QPs a
157 David's Compositions . . . . 11QPs a
158 Hymn to the Creator . . . . 11QPs a
159 Apostrophe to Zion . . . . 4QPs f
160 Plea for Deliverance . . . . 11QPs a
160 Plea for Deliverance . . . . 11QPs b
161 Apostrophe to Judah . . . . 4QPs f
162 Eschatological Hymn . . . . 4QPs f

PROVERBS

1:27-33 . . . . 4QProv a
2:1 . . . . 4QProv a
14:31-35 . . . . 4QProv b
15:1-5, 7-8, 20-31 . . . . 4QProv b

ECCLESIASTES

1:1-14 . . . . 4QQoh b
5:13-17 . . . . 4QQoh a
6:3-8 . . . . 4QQoh a
7:7-9 . . . . 4QQoh a

SONG OF SOLOMON

1:1-7 . . . . 6QCant
2:9-17 . . . . 4QCant b
3:1-2 . . . . 4QCant b
3:7-8 . . . . 4QCant c
3:7-8, 10-11 . . . . 4QCant a
4:1-7 . . . . 4QCant a
4:1-11, 14-16 . . . . 4QCant b
5:1 . . . . 4QCant b

ISAIAH

1:1-3 . . . . 4QIsa a
1:1-6 . . . . 4QIsa b
1:1-6 . . . . 4QIsa j
1:1-31 . . . . 1QIsa a
1:4-14 . . . . (2)Mur Isa
1:10-16, 18-31 . . . . 4QIsa f
2:1-3 . . . . 4QIsa f
2:1-4 . . . . 4QIsa l

13:4-6 . . . . 4QIsa a
14:1-5 . . . . 4QIsa c
14:1-12, 21-24 . . . . 4QIsa l
14:1-32 . . . . 1QIsa a
14:28-32 . . . . 4QIsa o
15:1 . . . . 4QIsa o
15:1-9 . . . . 1QIsa a
15:3-9 . . . . 1QIsa b
16:1-2, 7-11 . . . . 1QIsa b
16:1-14 . . . . 1QIsa a
16:7-8(?) . . . . 4QIsa o
17:1-14 . . . . 1QIsa a
17:8-14 . . . . 4QIsa b
17:9-14 . . . . 4QIsa a
18:1, 5-7 . . . . 4QIsa b
18:1-7 . . . . 1QIsa a
19:1-25 . . . . 1QIsa a
19:1-25 . . . . 4QIsa b
19:7-17, 20-25 . . . . 1QIsa b
19:9-14 . . . . 4QIsa a
20:1 . . . . 1QIsa b
20:1-4 . . . . 4QIsa b
20:1-6 . . . . 1QIsa a
20:1-6 . . . . 4QIsa a
20:4-6 . . . . 4QIsa f
21:1-2, 4-16 . . . . 4QIsa a
21:1-17 . . . . 1QIsa a
21:11-14 . . . . 4QIsa b
21:25 . . . . 4QIsa c
22:1-25 . . . . 1QIsa a
22:10-14 . . . . 4QIsa c
22:11-18, 24-25 . . . . 1QIsa b
22:13-25 . . . . 4QIsa a
22:15-22, 25 . . . . 4QIaa f
22:24-25 . . . . 4QIsa b
23:1-4 . . . . 1QIsa b
23:1-12 . . . . 4QIsa a
23:1-18 . . . . 1QIsa a
23:8-18 . . . . 4QIsa c
24:1-3 . . . . 4QIsa f
24:1-15, 19-23 . . . . 4QIsa c
24:1-23 . . . . 1QIsa a
24:2 . . . . 4QIsa b
24:18-23 . . . . 1QIsa b
25:1-2, 8-12 . . . . 4QIsa c
25:1-8 . . . . 1QIsa b
25:1-12 . . . . 1QIsa a

44:1-28	1QIsa a
44:19-28	4QIsa b
44:21-28	1QIsa b
45:1-4, 6-13	4QIsa c
45:1-13	1QIsa b
45:1-25	1QIsa a
45:20-25	4QIsa b
46:1-3	4QIsa b
46:1-13	1QIsa a
46:3-13	1QIsa b
46:10-13	4QIsa d
47:1-6, 8-9	4QIsa d
47:1-14	1QIsa b
47:1-15	1QIsa a
48:1-22	1QIsa a
48:8-22	4QIsa d
48:10-13, 17-19	4QIsa c
48:17-22	1QIsa b
49:1-15	1QIsa b
49:1-15	4QIsa d
49:1-26	1QIsa a
49:21-23	4QIsa b
50:1-11	1QIsa a
50:7-11	1QIsa b
50:7-11	4QIsa c
51:1-10	1QIsa b
51:1-16	4QIsa c
51:1-23	1QIsa a
51:14-16	4QIsa b
52:1-15	1QIsa a
52:2, 7	4QIsa b
52:4-7	4QIsa d
52:7-15	1QIsa b
52:10-15	4QIsa c
53:1-3, 6-8	4QIsa c
53:1-12	1QIsa a
53:1-12	1QIsa b
53:8-12	4QIsa d
53:11-12	4QIsa b
54:1-6	1QIsa b
54:1-11	4QIsa d
54:1-17	1QIsa a
54:3-17	4QIsa c
54:11-13	4QIsa q
55:1-6	4QIsa c
55:1-13	1QIsa a
55:2-13	1QIsa b

Manuscript listed in some publications but existence uncertain:
4QIsa r

JEREMIAH

9:22-26 . . . . 4QJer b
10:1-18 . . . . 4QJer b
10:9-14 . . . . 4QJer a
10:12-13 . . . . 4QJer c
11:3-6 . . . . 4QJer a
12:3-6, 13-17 . . . . 4QJer a
13:1-7 . . . . 4QJer a
14:4-7 . . . . 4QJer a
15:1-2 . . . . 4QJer a
17:8-26 . . . . 4QJer a
18:15-23 . . . . 4QJer a
19:1 . . . . 4QJer a
19:8-9(?) . . . . 4QJer c
20:1(?)-5, 7-9(?), 12(?)-15 . . . . 4QJer c
21:7-10 . . . . 4QJer c
22:4-6, 10-28 . . . . 4QJer c
22:4-16 . . . . 4QJer a
25:7-8, 15-17, 24-26 . . . . 4QJer c
26:10-13 . . . . 4QJer c
27:1-3, 13-15 . . . . 4QJer c
30:4(?)-24 . . . . 4QJer c
31:1-14, 15(?)-26 . . . . 4QJer c
33:16-20 . . . . 4QJer c
42:7-11, 14 . . . . 2QJer
43:2-10 . . . . 4QJer d
43:8-11 . . . . 2QJer
44:1-3, 12-14 . . . . 2QJer
46:27-28 . . . . 2QJer
47:1-7 . . . . 2QJer
48:7, 25-39, 43-45 . . . . 2QJer
49:10 . . . . 2QJer
50:4-6 . . . . 4QJer e

LAMENTATIONS

1:1-16 . . . . 4QLam
1:10-12 . . . . 3QLam
3:53-62 . . . . 3QLam
4:5-8, 11-15, 19-22 . . . . 5QLam a
4:17-19 . . . . 5QLam b
5:1-12 . . . . 5QLam a

EZEKIEL

1:10-13, 16-17, 20-24 . . . . 4QEzek b
4:3-5, 9-10 . . . . 11QEzek
4:16-17 . . . . 1QEzek

DANIEL

Manuscripts known to exist but contents not yet published:
4QDan d, 4QDan e

MINOR PROPHETS

Manuscript known to exist but contents not yet published:
4QXII g

HOSEA

1:7-9	4QXII d
2:1-5	4QXII d
2:13-15	4QXII c
3:2-4	4QXII c
4:1-19(?)	4QXII c
5:1	4QXII c
13:4-8, 15	4QXII c
13:15(?)	4QXII ?
14:1, 3-6	4QXII ?
14:1-6	4QXII c

JOEL

1:11-20	4QXII c
2:1, 10-19	4QXII c
2:20, 26-27	(2)MurXII
3:1-5	(2)MurXII
4:1-16	(2)MurXII
4:6-17	4QXII c

AMOS

1:3-5	5QXII
1:5-15	(2)MurXII
2:1	(2)MurXII
2:12-16	4QXII c
3:1-4	4QXII c
4:1-2	4QXII c
6:1	(2)MurXII
6:13-14	4QXII c
7:1-16	4QXII c
7:3-16	(2)MurXII
8:4-7, 11-14	(2)MurXII
9:1-15	(2)MurXII

OBADIAH

1-21	(2)MurXII

JONAH

1:1-2, 8-9, 16	4QXII a
1:1-16	(2)MurXII
1:6-8, 10-16	4QXII f
1:14-16	8Hev grXII
2:1-7	8Hev gkXII

3:1-2 . . . . 4QXII c
3:1-20 . . . . (2)MurXII
3:6-7 . . . . 8HevgkXII
3:19-20 . . . . 4QXII b

HAGGAI

1:1-2 . . . . 4QXII b
1:1-15 . . . . (2)MurXII
2:1-6, 10, 12-23 . . . . (2)MurXII
2:2-4 . . . . 4QXII b
2:20-21 . . . . 4QXII d

ZECHARIAH

1:1-4 . . . . (2)MurXII
1:4-6, 9-10, 13-14 . . . . 4QXII e
2:10-14 . . . . 4QXII e
3:4-10 . . . . 4QXII e
7:4-5(?) 7Q5
8:19-21, 23 . . . . 8Hev gkXII
9:1-5 . . . . 8Hev gkXII
14:18 . . . . 4Q XII a

MALACHI

1:1-4, 12-15 . . . . 8Hev gkXII
2:2-4, 6-12, 16-17 [=1:19–2:13 EVV] . . . . 8Hev gkXII
2:10-17(?) . . . . 4QXII a
3:1-2, 4-7 . . . . 8Hev gkXII
3:1-24 [=3:1–4:6 EVV] . . . . 4QXII a
3:6(?)-7 . . . . 4QXII c

SIRACH

51:13-30 . . . . 11QPs a

Bibliography

Albrektson, Bertil. 1975. "Textual Criticism and the Textual Basis of a Translation of the Old Testament." *The Bible Translator* 26:314–324.

_____. 1978. "Reflections on the Emergence of a Standard Text." In *Supplement to Vetus Testamentum 29*, 49–65.

_____. 1981. "Difficilior lectio probabilior." In *Remembering All the Way* (OTS, 21), 5–18.

Allegro, John Marco. 1965. *The Shapira Affair*. Garden City, N.Y.: Doubleday.

Allis, Oswald T. 1953. *Revised Version or Revised Bible? A Critique of the Revised Standard Version of the Old Testament* (1952). Philadelphia: Presbyterian and Reformed.

Andersen, Francis, and D. N. Freedman. 1989. "Another Look at *4QSam*[b]." *Revue de Qumran* 14:7–29.

Archer, Gleason L. 1981. "A Reassessment of the Value of the Septuagint of 1 Samuel for Textual Emendations, in the Light of Qumran Fragments." In *Tradition and Testament: Essays in Honor of Charles Lee Feinberg*, edited by John S. and Paul D. Feinberg, 223–240. Chicago: Moody.

Arichea, D. C. 1982. "Jeremiah and the UBS Hebrew Old Testament Text Project." *The Bible Translator* 33:101–106.

Avigad, N. 1958. "The Palaeography of the Dead Sea Scrolls and Related Documents." In *Aspects of the Dead Sea Scrolls*, edited by Chaim Rabin and Yigael Yadin, 56–87. Jerusalem: Magnes.

Báez-Camargo, Gonzalo. 1980. "The Dead Sea Scrolls and the Translator." *The Bible Translator* 31:438–443.

Baigent, Michael, and Richard Leigh. 1991. *The Dead Sea Scroll Deception*. New York: Summit.

Barkay, Gabriel. 1986. *Ketef Hinnom: A Treasury Facing Jerusalem's Walls*. Jerusalem: The Israel Museum.

Barker, Kenneth, ed. 1986. *The NIV: The Making of a Contemporary Translation*. Grand Rapids: Zondervan.

Barr, James. 1974. "After Five Years: A Retrospect on Two Major Translations of the Bible [NEB and NAB]." *Heythrop Journal* 15:381–405.

_____. 1979. *The Typology of Literalism in Ancient Biblical Translations*. Göttingen: Vandenhoeck & Ruprecht.

_____. 1986. "[Review of] Critique textuelle de l'Ancien Testament." *Journal of Theological Studies* 37:445–450.

Barr, James. 1988. "From Sacred Story to Sacred Text: Canon as Paradigm, by James A. Sanders." *Critical Review of Books in Religion*, 1988. Atlanta: Scholars Press.

Barthélemy, Dominique. 1982. *Critique textuelle de l'Ancien Testament*, 1. (Orbis Biblicus et Orientalis, 0⁄1). Fribourg and Göttingen: Editions Universitaires/Vandenhoeck und Ruprecht.

_____. 1976. "Text, Hebrew, history of." In *The Interpreter's Dictionary of the Bible,* supplementary vol. Nashville: Abingdon.

_____. 1984. "L'enchevtrement de l'histoire textuelle et de l'histoire littéraire dans les relations entre la Septante et le Texte Massorétique." In *De Septuaginta: Studies in honour of John William Wevers*, edited by Albert Pietersma and Claude Cox, 19–40.

Barthélemy, Dominique, David W. Gooding, Johan Lust, and Emanuel Tov. 1986. *The story of David and Goliath. Textual and literary criticism* (Orbis Biblicus et Orientalis, 73). Fribourg and Göttingen: Fribourg U. Press and Vandenhoeck & Ruprecht.

Birnbaum, Solomon A. 1950. "The Leviticus Fragments from the Cave." *Bulletin of the American Schools of Oriental Research* 118:20–27.

_____. 1952. *The Qumrân (Dead Sea) Scrolls and Palaeography.* (BASOR Supplementary Studies, 13–14). New Haven, Conn.: American Schools of Oriental Research.

Bonani, G. et al. 1991. "Radiocarbon Dating of the Dead Sea Scrolls." *Atiqot* 20:27–32.

Borbone, Pier Giorgio. 1984. "La critica del testo e l'Antico Testamento ebraico: A proposito di un libro recente [Barthélemy, Critque textuelle]." *Rivista di Storia e Letteratura Religiosa* 20:251–274.

Bratcher, Robert G. 1979. "The Hebrew Old Testament Text Project and the Translator." *The Bible Translator* 30:326–332.

Brock, Sebastian P. 1966. "The recensions of the LXX version of 1 Samuel." dissertation, Oxford University.

_____. 1985, 1987. "[Reviews of] Dominique Barthélemy, Critique textuelle de l'Ancien Testament 1, 2." *Journal of Jewish Studies* 36:107–109; 38:242–243.

Brockington, L. H. 1973. *The Hebrew text of the Old Testament: the readings adopted by the translators of the New English Bible*. Oxford & Cambridge: University Presses.

Brownlee, William H. 1963. "The Scroll of Ezekiel from the Eleventh Qumran Cave." *Revue de Qumran* 4:11–28.

_____. 1964. *The Meaning of the Qumrân Scrolls for the Bible with special attention to the Book of Isaiah*. New York: Oxford University Press.

Burrows, Millar. 1955. *The Dead Sea Scrolls*. New York: Viking.

_____. 1958. *More Light on the Dead Sea Scrolls*. New York: Viking.

_____. 1964. *Diligently Compared: The Revised Standard Version and the King James Version of the Old Testament*. New York and London: Thomas Nelson.

Charlesworth, James H. et al. 1992. *Graphic Concordance to the Dead Sea Scrolls*. Louisville, Ky.: Westminster/John Knox.

Clark, David J. 1984. "The Influence of the Dead Sea Scrolls on Modern Translations of Isaiah." *The Bible Translator* 35:122–130.

Cook, Johann. 1989. "The Computerized Data Base for the Dead Sea Biblical Scrolls." In *Bible and Computer: Methods, Tools, Results*. Paris/Geneva: Champion-Slatkine, 213–221.

Cross, Frank M. 1953. "A New Qumran Biblical Fragment Related to the Original Hebrew Underlying the Septuagint." *Bulletin of the American Schools of Oriental Research* 132:15–26.

_____. 1955. "The Oldest Manuscripts from Qumran." *Journal of Biblical Literature* 74:147–172.

_____. 1956. "A Report on the Biblical Fragments of Cave 4." *Bulletin of the American Schools of Oriental Research* 141:9–13.

_____. 1961. "The Development of the Jewish Scripts." In *The Bible and the Ancient Near East: Essays in Honor of W. F. Albright*, 133–202. Garden City, N.Y.: Doubleday.

_____. 1961b. *The Ancient Library of Qumran and Modern Biblical Studies*, rev. ed. Garden City, N.Y.: Doubleday.

_____. 1968. "The Song of the Sea and Canaanite Myth." *Journal for Theology and the Church* 5:1–25.

_____. 1983. "Studies in the Structure of Hebrew Verse: The Prosody of Lamentations 1:1-22." In *The Word of the Lord Shall Go Forth,* edited by Carol Meyers and M. O'Connor. Winona Lake, Ind.: Eisenbrauns, 129–155.

_____. 1985. "New Directions in Dead Sea Scroll Research. I: The Text Behind the Text of the Hebrew Bible." *Bible Review* 1, no. 2:12–25.

_____, and Shemaryahu Talmon. 1975. *Qumran and the History of the Biblical Text*. Cambridge, Mass.: Harvard University.

Crotty, Robert. 1970. "NEB—The Book of Samuel." *Australian Biblical Review* 18:16–20.

Davila, James. 1988. *Unpublished Pentateuchal Manuscripts from Cave IV, Qumran: 4QGenEx[a], 4QGen[b-h, j-k]*. Dissertation, Harvard University.

_____. 1990. "New Qumran Readings from Genesis One." *Of Scribes and Scrolls*, edited by Harold W. Attridge, *et al.*, 3–11. Lanham, Md.: University Press of America.

_____. 1991. "The Name of God at Moriah: An Unpublished Fragment from 4QGenExod[a]." *JBL* 110:577–582.

Deist, F. E. 1988. *Witnesses to the Old Testament: Introducing Old Testament Textual Criticism*. Pretoria: NG Kerkboekhandel.

Dillard, Raymond B. 1985. "David's Census: Perspectives on 2 Samuel 24 and 1 Chronicles 21." In *Through Christ's Word: A Festschrift for Dr. Philip E. Hughes,* edited by W. Robert Godfrey and Jesse Boyd, 94–107. Phillipsburg, N.J.: Presbyterian and Reformed.

Duncan, Julie. 1989. *A Critical Editon of Deuteronomy Manuscripts from Qumran. Cave IV: 4QDt[b], 4QDt[e], 4QDt[h], 4QDt[j], 4QDt[k], 4QDt[l]*. Dissertation, Harvard University.

Eisenman, Robert H., and James M. Robinson, eds. 1991. *A Facsimile Edition of the Dead Sea Scrolls*. 2 vols. Washington, D.C.: Biblical Archaeology Society.

Ellington, John. 1989. "Old Testament Textual Problems: a Pragmatic Approach for Nonscholars." *Notes on Translation 3,* 2:4–29.

Eshel, Esther. 1991. "4QDeut^n—A Text that Has Undergone Harmonistic Editing." *Hebrew Union College Annual* 62:117–154.

Eybers, I. H. 1960. "Notes on the Texts of Samuel Found in Qumran Cave 4." In *Studies on the Books of Samuel*, 1–17. Pretoria: Die Ou Testamentiese Werkgemeenskap in Suid-Afrika.

Fitzmyer, Joseph A. 1990. *The Dead Sea Scrolls: Major Publications and Tools for Study*. Rev. ed. Atlanta: Scholars Press.

_____. 1992. *Responses to 101 Questions on the Dead Sea Scrolls*. New York/Mahwah: Paulist.

Fokkelman, J. P. 1986. *Narrative art and poetry in the books of Samuel, volume 2: The crossing fates (I Sam. 13-31 & II Sam. 1)*. Appendix I: Accounting for the selected text, 717–740. Aasen: van Goricum.

Francisco, Clyde T. "Revised Standard Version of the Old Testament." *Review and Expositor* 50:30–55.

Freedman, David N. 1962. "The Massoretic Text and the Qumran Scrolls." *Textus* 2:87–102.

_____. 1974. "Variant Readings in the Leviticus Scroll from Qumran Cave 11." *CBQ* 36:525–534.

_____, and K. A. Mathews. 1985. *The Paleo-Hebrew Leviticus Scroll (11QpaleoLev)*. Winona Lake, Ind.: Eisenbrauns, for American Schools of Oriental Research.

Fuller, Russell. 1988. *The Minor Prophets Manuscripts from Qumrân, Cave IV*. Dissertation, Harvard University.

_____. 1991. "Text-Critical Problems in Malachi 2:10-16." *JBL* 110:47–57.

_____. 1991. "A Critical Note on Hosea 12:10 and 13:4 [4Qxii^c]." *Revue Biblique* 98:343–357

García Martínez, Florentino. 1989. "Lista de MSS procedentes de Qumran." *Henoch* 11:149–232.

_____. 1989. "Estudios Qumranicos 1975-1985: Panorama Critico (VI)." *Estudios Bíblicos* 47:225–267.

_____. 1992. "Texts from Qumran Cave 11." In *The Dead Sea Scrolls: Forty Years of Research*, edited by Devorah Dimant and Uriel Rappaport, 18–26. Leiden/Jerusalem: Brill/ Magnes.

Golb, Norman. 1980. "The Problem of Origin and Identification of the Dead Sea Scrolls." *Proceedings of the American Philosophical Society* 124:1–24.

Gordon, Robert P. 1975. "The Citation of the Targums in Recent English Translations (RSV, JB, NEB)." *Journal of Jewish Studies* 26:50–60.

Goshen-Gottstein, Moshe. 1967. "Hebrew biblical manuscripts, their history and their place in the HUBP Edition." *Biblica* 48:243–290.

_____. 1988. "The Book of Samuel—Hebrew and Greek—Hindsight of a Century." *Textus* 14:147–161.

_____. 1992. "The Development of the Hebrew Text of the Bible: Theories and Practice of Textual Criticism." *Vetus Testamentum* 42:204–212.

Greenspoon, Leonard. 1989. "It's All Greek to Me: The Septuagint in Modern English Versions of the Hebrew Bible." In *VII Congress of the International Organization for Septuagint and Cognate Studies: Leuven 1989,* edited by Claude E. Cox. Atlanta: Scholars Press, 1–21.

_____. 1992. "The Qumran Fragments of Joshua: Which Puzzle are They Part of and Where Do They Fit?" In *Septuagint, Scrolls and Cognate Writings*, George J. Brooke and Barnabas Lindars, editors, 159–194. Atlanta: Scholars.

Hanhart, Robert. 1985. "[Review of] Dominique Barthélemy, Critique textuelle de l'Ancien Testament." *Göttingische Gelehrte Anzeigen* 237:143–149.

Hanson, Richard S. 1964. "Paleo-Hebrew Scripts in the Hasmonean Age." *Bulletin of the American Schools of Oriental Reserach* 175:26–42.

Harrelson, Walter. 1990. "Textual and Translation Problems in the Book of Esther." *Perspectives in Religious Studies* 17:197–208.

Harris, R. Laird. 1955–56. "The Evidence for the Canon from the Dead Sea Scrolls." *Reformation Review* 3:139-153.

Hart, David H. 1990. "Some Recent Approaches to the History of the Biblical Text," unpublished paper presented at Society of Biblical Literature meeting in 1990.

Hartley, John E. 1992. *Leviticus* Word Biblical Commentary, vol. 4. Waco: Word Books.

Hayes, John H. 1987. "Historical Reconstruction, Textual Emendation, and Biblical Translation: Some Examples from the RSV." *Perspectives in Religious Studies* 14:5–9.

Hoegenhaven, Jesper. 1984. "The First Isaiah Scroll from Qumran (1QIs[a]) and the Massoretic Text. Some Reflections with Special Regard to Isaiah 1–12." *Journal for the Study of the Old Testament* 28:17–35.

Horgan, Maurya P. 1979. *Pesharim: Qumran Interpretations of Biblical Books.* The Catholic Biblical Quarterly Monograph Series, 8. Washington, D.C.: Catholic Biblical Association.

Irwin, W. A. 1954. "Textual Criticism and Old Testament Translation." *The Bible Translator* 5:54–58.

Janzen, J. Gerald. 1973. *Studies in the Text of Jeremiah.* Harvard Semitic Monographs, no. 6. Cambridge, Mass.: Harvard University.

Jastram, Nathan R. 1990. *The Book of Numbers from Qumran, Cave IV (4QNum[b]).* Dissertation, Harvard University.

Johnson, Bo. 1963. *Die hexaplarische Rezension des 1. Samuelbuches der Septuaginta.* Studia Theologica Lundensia, no. 22. Lund: CWK Gleerup.

_____. 19– . "On the Masoretic Text at the Beginning of the First Book of Samuel." *Svensk Exegetisk Årsbok* :130–137.

Klein, Ralph W. 1985. "[Review of] Critique textuelle de l'Ancien Testament, 1." *Journal of Biblical Literature* 104:137–138.

Kraft, Robert, ed. 1972. "Symposium: The Methodology of Textual Criticism in Jewish Greek Scriptures, with Special Attention to the Problems in Samuel—Kings." In *1972 Proceedings* [IOSCS Symposium, 1972], edited by Robert Kraft. Los Angeles: IOSCS and Society of Biblical Literature, 2–126.

Locher, Clemens. 1977–78. "Der Psalter der 'Einheitsübersetzung' und die Textkritik I, II." *Biblica* 58:313–341; 59:49–79.

Luke, K. 1986. "A Verse Missing from 1 Samuel 10:27–11:15." *Bible Bhashyam* 12:196–212.

Lust, Johan. 1986. "Ezekiel Manuscripts in Qumran. Preliminary Edition of 4QEz a and b." In *Ezekiel and his Book,* edited by J. Lust. Leuven: Peeters, 90–100.

Maass, F. 1956. "Zu den Qumran-Varianten der Bücher Samuel." *Theologische Literaturzeitung* 81:cols. 337–340.

Mansoor, Menahem. 1959. "The Case of Shapira's Dead Sea (Deuteronomy) Scroll of 1883." *Transactions of the Wisconsin Academy of Sciences, Arts and Letters* 47:183–229.

Maori, Yeshayahu. 1992. "The Text of the Hebrew Bible in Rabbinic Writings in the Light of the Qumran Evidence." In *The Dead Sea Scrolls: Forty Years of Research*, edited by Devorah Dimant and Uriel Rappaport, 283–289. Leiden/Jerusalem: Brill/Magnes.

Martin, John A. 1984. "The Text of 1 and 2 Samuel." *Bibliotheca Sacra* 141:209–222.

Martin, Malachi. 1958. *The Scribal Character of the Dead Sea Scrolls,* 2 vols. Louvain: Publications Universitaires/Institut Orientaliste.

McCarter, P. Kyle. 1980. *I Samuel* The Anchor Bible, vol. 8. Garden City, N.Y.: Doubleday.

_____. 1984. *II Samuel* The Anchor Bible, 9. Garden City, N.Y.: Doubleday.

_____. 1986. *Textual Criticism: Recovering the Text of the Hebrew Bible.* Philadelphia: Fortress.

McLean, M. D. 1982. *The Use and Development of Paleo-Hebrew in the Hellenistic and Roman Period.* Dissertation, Harvard University.

Mertens, Alfred. 1971. *Das Buch Daniel im Lichte der Texte vom Toten Meer.* Echter: KBW Verlag.

Milik, J. T. 1966. "Fragment d'une source du psautier (4Q Ps 89) et fragments des Jubilés, du Document de Damas, d'un phylactère dans la grotte 4 de Qumrân." *Revue Biblique* 73:94–106.

Morrow, Francis J. 1973. *The Text of Isaiah at Qumran.* Dissertation, Catholic University, Washington, D.C.

Muilenberg, James. 1954. "A Qoheleth Scroll from Qumran." *BASOR* 135:20–28.

Müller, Mogens. 1989. *"Hebraica sive Graeca Veritas:* The Jewish Bible at the Time of the New Testament and the Christian Bible." *Scandanavian Journal of the Old Testament* 2(1989):55–71.

O'Callaghan, José. 1972. *New Testament Papyri in Qumrân Cave 7?* (Supplement to *JBL*, vol. 91). English translation of the original Spanish article that appeared in *Biblica* 53(1972):91-100.

Orlinsky, Harry M. 1974. "The New Jewish Version of the Torah: Toward a New Philosophy of Bible Translation." In *Essays in Biblical Culture amd Bible Translation*, 396–417. New York: Ktav.

_____, ed. 1970. *Notes on the New Translation of the Torah.* Philadelphia: Jewish Publication Society.

Osborn, Noel D. 1981. "Exodus and the HOTTP." Unpublished paper presented at the UBS Triennial Translations Workshop, Chania, Crete, May 1981.

Payne, D. F. 1974. "Old Testament Textual Criticism: Its Principles and Practice. Apropos of Recent English Versions." *Tyndale Bulletin* 25:99–112.

Peters, Paul W. "Variants of the Isaiah Scroll Adopted by the Revised Standard Version and the Jerusalem Bible." *Wisconsin Lutheran Quarterly* 71:134–138; 209–223.

Pisano, Stephen. 1984. *Additions or Omissions in the Books of Samuel. The significant pluses and minuses in the Massoretic, LXX, and Qumran texts* (Orbis Biblicus et Orientalis, 57). Freiburg and Göttingen: Freiburg University Press/Vandenhoeck & Ruprecht.

_____. *Preliminary and Interim Report on the Hebrew Old Testament Text Project. 1973–1980.* 5 volumes. London: United Bible Societies.

Puech, E. 1980. "Fragment d'un roleau de la Genèse provenant du Désert de Juda" (Gen. 33:18–34:3). *Revue de Qumran* 10:163–166.

_____. 1990. "11QPsAp^a: un rituel d'exorcismes. Essai de reconstruction." *Revue de Qumran* 14:377–408.

Reed, Stephen A. 1991. "Survey of the Dead Sea Scrolls Fragments and Photographs at the Rockefeller Museum." *Biblical Archaeologist* 54:44–51.

_____. 1991–92. *Dead Sea Scroll Inventory Project: Lists of Documents, Photographs, and Museum Plates.* In 14 fascicles. Claremont, Calif.: Ancient Biblical Manuscript Center.

_____. *The Revision of the Old Testament: Opinions of eminent German Hebraists on the revision of the Massoretic text, published for the use of the American Committee.* 1886. New York: Charles Scribner's.

Roberts, C. H. 1936. *Two Biblical Papyri.* Manchester: Manchester University Press.

Rofé, Alexander. 1982. "The Acts of Nahash according to 4QSam^a." *Israel Exploration Journal* 32:129–133.

Rosenbloom, J. R. 1970. *The Dead Sea Isaiah Scroll: A Literary Analysis. A Comparison with the Masoretic Text and the Biblia Hebraica.* Grand Rapids: Eerdmans.

Rüger, H. P. 1979. "The Hebrew Old Testament Text Project: A Response [to the article by Bratcher in the same issue]." *The Bible Translator* 30:333–336.

Samuel, Athanasius Yeshue. 1966. *Treasure of Qumran: My Story of the Dead Sea Scrolls.* Philadelphia: Westminster.

Sanders, J. A. 1967. *The Dead Sea Psalms Scroll.* Ithaca, N.Y.: Cornell University.

_____. 1971. "Text Criticism and the NJV Torah." *Journal of the American Academy of Religion* 39:193–197.

_____. 1987. *From Sacred Story to Sacred Text.* Philadelphia: Fortress.

_____. 1987. "The Hermeneutics of Text Criticism and Translation." Paper delivered at the SBL Meeting, Boston, 7 December 1987.

_____. 1991. "Stability and Fluidity in Text and Canon." In *Tradition of the Text. Studies offered to Dominique Barthélemy in Celebration of his 70th Birthday,* edited by Gerald J. Norton and Stephen Pisano, 203–217.

Sanderson, Judith. 1986. *An Exodus Scroll from Qumran: 4QpaleoExod^m and the Samaritan Tradition* (Harvard Semitic Studies, 20). Atlanta: Scholars.

Sarna, N. M. 1972. "Bible Text." *Encyclopedia Judaica,* vol. 4, cols. 832–836.

Scanlin, Harold P. 1988. "What Is the Canonical Shape of the Old Testament Text We Translate?" In *Issues in Bible Translation,* edited by Philip C. Stine, 207–220. London: United Bible Societies.

_____. *Scrolls from the Wilderness of the Dead Sea.* 1965. Berkeley, Calif.: University of California for the American Schools of Oriental Research. (The

1969 printing omitted several pages of front matter and, as a result, references are lower by two pages.)

Shanks, Hershel, ed. 1992. *Understanding the Dead Sea Scrolls. A Reader from the Biblical Archaeology Review.* New York: Random House.

Sinclair, Lawrence A. 1990. "11QPs[a]: A Psalm Scroll from Qumran: Text and Canon." In *The Psalms and Other Studies on the Old Testament presented to Joseph I. Hunt,* edited by Jack Knight and Lawrence Sinclair, 109–115. Nashotah, Wis.: Nashotah House Seminary.

_____. 1989. "A Qumran Biblical Fragment *4QEzek*[a] (Ezek. 10:17–11:11)." *Revue de Qumran* 14:99–105.

Skehan, Patrick W. 1954. "A Fragment of the 'Song of Moses' (Deut. 32) from Qumran." *BASOR* 136:12–15.

_____. 1957. "The Qumran Manuscripts and Textual Criticism." In *Volume du Congrès: Strasbourg, 1956,* Leiden: Brill, 148–160.

_____. 1964. "A Psalm Manuscript from Qumran" (4QPs[b]). *CBQ* 26:313–322.

_____. 1969. "The Scrolls and the Old Testament Text." In *New Directions in Biblical Archaeology,* 89–100. Garden City, N.Y.: Doubleday.

_____. 1977. "4QLXXNum: A Pre-Christian Reworking of the Septuagint." *Harvard Theological Review* 70:39–50.

_____. 1978. "Qumran and Old Testament Criticism [with] Appendix: Collation of 4Q Psalm MSS against BHS." In *Qumrân. Sa piété, sa théologie et son milieu,* edited by M. Delcor Paris-Gembloux/Lueven: Duculot/Leuven U. Press, 163–182.

_____. 1979. "Littérature de Qumrân.—A. Textes bibliques." In *Dictionnaire de la Bible. Supplément 9,* cols. 805–822.

_____. 1981. "Gleanings from Psalm Texts from Qumrân." In *Mélanges bibliques et orientaux en l'honneur de M. Henri Cazelles,* 439–452. Kevelaer: Butzen & Bercker.

Smith, Henry Preserved. 1885. "The Old Testament Text and the Revised Version." *The Presbyterian Review* 6:623–65.

Sollamo, Raija. 1986. "The Source Text for the [Finnish] Translation of the Old Testament." *The Bible Translator* 37:319–322.

Spottorno, Victoria. 1992. "Una nueva posible identificación de 7Q5." *Sefarad* 52:541–543.

Stegemann, Hartmut. 1990. "Methods for the Reconstruction of Scrolls from Scattered Fragments." In *Archaeology and History in the Dead Sea Scrolls,* edited by Lawrence H. Schiffman. Sheffield: JSOT Press.

Tal, Abraham. 1985. "[Review of] Dominique Barthélemy, Critique textuelle de l'Ancien Testament, 1." *Journal of Semitic Studies* 30:285–289.

Talmon, Shemaryahu. 1970. "The Old Testament Text." In *The Cambridge History of the Bible,* vol. 1, edited by P. R. Ackroyd and C. F. Evans, 159–199. Cambridge: University Press.

_____. 1989. "Fragments of Writings Written in Hebrew at Masada" [In Hebrew]. *Eretz Israel* 20:278–286.

_____. "Tekstkritiske bemaerkninger til oversaettelsen: Frste Samuelsbog." 1986. In *Samuels bgerne & Konge bgerne,* 277–285. Danish Bible Society.

_____. *Textual Notes on the New American Bible.* 1970. Paterson, N.J.: St. Anthony's Guild. (This important collection of textual notes appears in some early printings of the St. Anthony's Guild edition of the *New American Bible* and was also published separately. The text-critical notes do not appear in the footnotes of the *NAB*.)

Thackeray, H. St. John. 1929. *Josephus, the Man and the Historian.* Cincinnati, Ohio: Hebrew Union College. See especially "Josephus and Judaism: His Biblical Text," 75–99.

Thiede, Carsten Peter. 1992. *The Earliest Gospel Manuscript? The Qumran Papyrus 7Q5 and Its Significance for New Testament Studies.* London: Paternoster.

Thenius, Otto. 1898. *Die Bücher Samuels* (Kurzgefasstes exegetisches Handbuch zum Alten Testament), 3d ed., edited by Max Löhr. Leipzig: S. Hirzel.

Tov, Emanuel, ed. 1980. *The Hebrew and Greek Texts of Samuel* (Proceedings of the IOSCS, 1980). Jerusalem: Academon.

_____. 1982. "A Modern Textual Outlook Based on the Qumran Scrolls." *Hebrew Union College Annual* 53:11–27.

_____. 1985. "The Composition of 1 Samuel 16–18 in the Light of the Septuagint Version." In *Empirical Models for Biblical Criticism*, edited by Jeffrey H. Tigay. 97–130. Philadelphia: University of Pennsylvania.

_____. 1986. "The Orthography and Language of Hebrew Scrolls Found at Qumran and the Origin of These Scrolls." *Textus* 13:31-57.

_____. 1986. "The Growth of the Book of Joshua in the Light of the Evidence of the LXX Translation." In *Studies in Bible. 1986* (Scripta Hierosolymitana, 31), edited by Sara Japhet, 321–339.

_____. 1988. "Hebrew Biblical Manuscripts from the Judaean Desert: Their Contribution to Textual Criticism." *Journal of Jewish Studies* 1988:5–37.

_____. 1989. "The Jeremiah Scrolls from Cave 4." *Revue de Qumran* 14:189–206.

_____. 1991. "4QJer[c] (4Q72)." In *Tradition of the Text,* edited by Gerard J. Norton and Stephen Pisano. Fribourg and Göttingen: Fribourg University Press/Vandenhoeck & Ruprecht. 249–276, plates 1–7.

_____. 1992. *Textual Criticism of the Hebrew Bible.* Minneapolis and Assen/Maastricht: Fortress/Van Goricum. (Revised and enlarged edition of the 1989 Hebrew edition) Jerusalem: Bialik.

_____. 1992. "4QLev[d] (4Q26)." In *The Scriptures and the Scrolls: Studies in honour of A. S. van der Woude on the occasion of his 65th birthday,* edited by F. Garcia Martina et al., 1–5. Leiden: E. J. Brill.

_____. 1992c. "The Textual Base of the Corrections in the Biblical Text." In *The Dead Sea Scrolls: Forty Years of Research*, edited by Devorah Dimant and Uriel Rappaport, 299–314. Leiden/Jerusalem: Brill/Magnes.

_____. 1992. "Three Fragments of Jeremiah from Qumran Cave 4." *Revue de Qumran* 15:531–541.

Trebolle, Barrera J. 1989. "Textual Variants in 4QJudg[a] and the Textual and Editorial History of the Book of Judges." *Revue de Qumran* 14:229–245.

_____. 1991. "Édition Préliminaire de *4QJuges[b].*" *Revue de Qumran* 15:79–100.

_____. 1992. "Light from 4QJudg[a] and 4QKgs[a] on the Text of Judges and Kings." In *The Dead Sea Scrolls: Forty Years of Research*, edited by Devorah Dimant and Uriel Rappaport, 315–324. Leiden/Jerusalem: E. J. Brill/Magnes.

_____. 1992. "Édition préliminaire de *4QChroniques*." *Revue de Qumran* 15:523–528.

Trever, John C. 1965. *The Untold Story of Qumran*. Westwood, N.J.: Fleming H. Revell.

_____. 1965. "Completion of the Publication of Some Fragments from Qumran Cave I." *Revue de Qumran* 5:323–336.

_____. 1970. "1Q Dan[a], the Latest of the Qumran Manuscripts." *Revue de Qumran* 7:277–286.

Ulrich, Eugene Charles. 1978. *The Qumran Text of Samuel and Josephus*. (Harvard Semitic Monographs, 19). Missoula, Mont.: Scholars.

_____. 1979. "4QSam[c]: A Fragmentary Manuscript of 2 Samuel 14–15 from the Scribe of the *Serek Hay-yahad* (1QS)." *BASOR* 235:1–25.

_____. 1984. "The Greek Manuscripts of the Pentateuch from Qumrân, including Newly-identified fragments of Deuteronomy (4qQLXXDeut)." In *De Septuaginta: Studies in Honour of John William Wevers on his 65th Birthday*, edited by Albert Pietersma and Claude Cox, 71–82. Mississauga, Ont.: Benben.

_____. 1987. "Daniel Manuscripts from Qumran. Part 1: A Preliminary Edition of 4QDan[a]." *Bulletin of the American Schools of Oriental Research*, 268:17–37.

_____. 1988. "Double Literary Editions of Biblical Narratives and Reflections on Determining the Form to Be Translated." In *Perspectives on the Hebrew Bible: Essays in Honor of Walter J. Harrelson*, edited by James L. Crenshaw, 101–116. Macon, Ga.: Mercer University Press.

_____. 1989. "Josephus' Biblical Text for the Books of Samuel." In *Josephus, the Bible and history*, edited by Louis H. Feldman and Gohei Hata, 81–96. Detroit: Wayne State U. Press.

_____. 1989. "The Biblical Scrolls from Qumran Cave 4: A Progress Report of their Publications." *Revue de Qumran* 14:207-228.

_____. 1989. "Daniel Manuscripts from Qumran. Part 2: Preliminary Editions of 4QDan[b] and 4QDan[c]." *Bulletin of the American Schools of Oriental Research* 274:3–26.

_____. 1990. "A Greek Paraphrase of Exodus on Papyrus from Qumran Cave 4." In *Studien zur Septuaginta—Robert Hanhart zu Ehren*, edited by Detlef Fraenkel et al., 287–298. Göttingen: Vandenhoeck & Ruprecht.

_____. 1992. "The Canonical Process, Textual Criticism, and Latter Stages in the Composition of the Bible." In *"Sha[c]arey Talmon" Studies in the Bible, Qumran and the Ancient Near East*, edited by Michael Fishbane and Emanuel Tov, 267–291. Winona Lake, Ind.: Eisenbrauns.

_____. 1992. "Ezra and Qoheleth Manuscripts from Qumran (4QEzra and 4QQoh[a,b])." In *Priests, Prophets and Scribes*, Eugene Ulrich, et al., eds., 139–157. Sheffield: JSOT Press.

_____, et al. forthcoming. *Qumran Cave Four: Vol. 4. Paleo-Hebrew and Greek Biblical Manuscripts*. Oxford: University Press.

van der Ploeg, J. P. M. 1967. "Fragments d'un Psautier de Qumrân (11QPs[b]) [now designated 11QPs[d]]." *Revue Biblique* 74:408–413.

_____. 1973. "Fragments d'un Psautier de Qumrân." In *Symbolae biblicae et mesopotamicae F.M.T. de Liagre Böhl dedicatae*, 308–309. Leiden: Brill.

_____. 1985–87. "Les manuscrits de la grotte XI de Qumrân." *Revue de Qumran* 12:3–15.

Vaux, Roland de. 1973. *Archaeology and the Dead Sea Scrolls*. London: British Academy.

_____. 1978. "Qumran, Khirbet—'Ein Feshkha." In *Encyclopedia of Archaeological Excavations in the Holy Land,* edited by Michael Avi-Yonah and Ephraim Stern, 978–986. Englewood Cliffs, N.J.: Prentice-Hall.

Vermes, Geza. 1987. "Biblical Studies and the Dead Sea Scrolls 1947–1987, Retrospects and Prospects." *Journal for the Study of the Old Testament* 39:113–128.

Waard, Jan de. 1965. *A Comparative Study of the Old Testament Text in the Dead Sea Scrolls and in the New Testament* (Studies on the Texts of the Desert of Judah, 4). Leiden: Brill.

Walters, Stanley D. 1988. "Hannah and Anna: The Greek and Hebrew Texts of 1 Samuel 1." *Journal of Biblical Literature* 107:385–412.

Waltke, Bruce. 1976. "The textual criticism of the Old Testament." In *Expositor's Bible Commentary,* vol. 1, 211–228. Grand Rapids: Zondervan.

Waltke, Bruce K. 1989. "The New International Version and Its Textual Principles in the Book of Psalms." *Journal of the Evangelical Theological Society* 32:17–26.

Weingreen, J. 1964. "A Rabbinic-Type Gloss in the LXX Version of 1 Samuel 1:18." *Vetus Testamentum* 14:225–228.

Wellhausen, Julius. 1872. *Der Text der Bücher Samuelis*. Göttingen: Vandenhoeck & Ruprecht.

Wevers, John Wm. 1988. "Barthélemy and Proto-Septuagint Studies." *Bulletin of the International Organization for Septuagint and Cognate Studies* 21:23–34.

White, Sidnie Ann. 1988. *A Critical Edition of Seven Manuscripts of Deuteronomy: 4QDt[a], 4QDt[c], 4QDt[d], 4QDt[f], 4QDt[g], 4QDt[l], and 4QDt[n]*. Dissertation, Harvard University.

_____. 1990. "The All Souls Deuteronomy and the Decalogue." *Journal of Biblical Literature* 109:193–206.

_____. 1990b. "4QDt[n]: Biblical Manuscript or Excerpted Text?" *Of Scribes and Scrolls*, edited by Harold W. Attridge et al., 31–20. Lanham, Md.: University Press of America.

_____. 1991. "Special Features of Four Biblical Manuscripts from Cave IV, Qumran: 4QDt[a], 4QDt[c], 4QDt[d], and 4QDt[g]." *Revue de Qumran* 15:157–167.

Whitworth, J. H. 1953. "Textual Emendations Used in the RSV OT." *Asbury Seminarian* 7:9–15.

Yadin, Yigael. 1957. *The Message of the Scrolls*. New York: Simon and Schuster.

_____. 1977. "Masada." In *Encyclopedia of Archaeological Excavations in the Holy Land,* edited by Michael Avi-Yonah and E. Stern, 793–816, especially 812ff. Englewood Cliffs, N.J.: Prentice-Hall.

Yardeni, Ada. 1990. "The Palaeography of 4QJer[a]—A Comparative Study." *Textus* 15:233–268.

Ziegler, Joseph. 1959. "Die Vorlage der Isaias-Septuaginta (LXX) und die erste Isaias-Rolle von Qumran (1QIs[a])." *Journal of Biblical Literature* 78:34–59.

Map of Dead Sea and Qumran Area

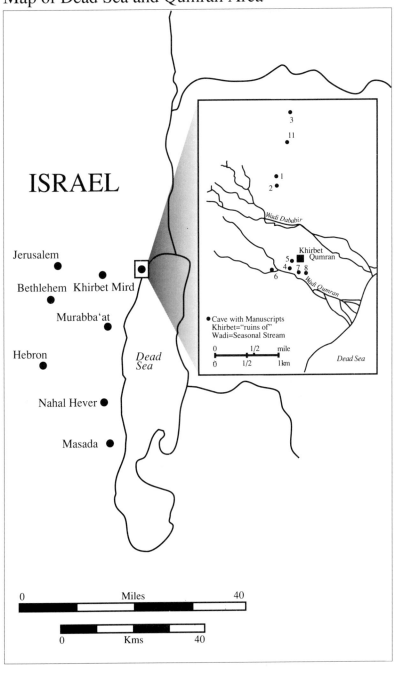

ISRAEL

Jerusalem

Bethlehem   Khirbet Mird

Murabba'at

Hebron

Dead Sea

Nahal Hever

Masada

3
11
1
2

Wadi Dababir

Khirbet Qumran
5
4 7 8
6

Wadi Qumran

● Cave with Manuscripts
Khirbet="ruins of"
Wadi=Seasonal Stream

0   1/2   mile
0   1/2   1km

Dead Sea

0   Miles   40

0   Kms   40

Photo 1: 1QIsa[a] is the best preserved of all the manuscripts discovered at Qumran. It is practically complete and is older by about 1,000 years than any other known Hebrew manuscript of a complete Old Testament book. The scroll is opened to columns xxxii and xxxiii, containing Isaiah 38:4–40:28. Isaiah 38:21-22 was inadvertently omitted by the scribe. These verses have been added and extend vertically

into the margin. Another correction has been made beginning on line seven in the left-hand column. Midway through the line the scribe jumped ahead from Isaiah 40:7 to 40:8. His eye dropped down a line because the word *tsyts* (flower) is repeated. When the error was discovered, dots were placed on the words that were incorrect and the rest of verse seven was added above the line and in the margin.

Photo 2: 1QIsa[b]: The center column contains portions of Isaiah 46:3–47:14. Portions of the preceding and following columns are also pictured. The scribe copied the scroll with great care. The text of 1QIsa[b] is quite close to the Masoretic Text.

Photo 3 (above): 1QpHab, column 10. Line 2 cites Habakkuk 2:10b; line 3 begins with the Hebrew word *pshrw* (its interpretation). In lines 7 and 14 the divine name is written in paleo-Hebrew characters.

Photo 4 (right): 4QpaleoExod^m, column xxxviii. This section begins at Exodus 32:10 and includes fragments through 32:30. The paleo-Hebrew script seen in this manuscript is similar to the script used in inscriptions coming from the period of the Divided Monarchy. The use of paleo-Hebrew in the biblical manuscripts from Qumran is not necessarily an indication that they are older. Almost all of the manuscripts written in paleo-Hebrew script are biblical texts, although a few fragments of biblical paraphrases used the script as well.

Photo 5: Papyrus fragments, including 4QIsa^p. The cross-hatch pattern of papyrus is visible. Papyrus tended to break into small fragments, making their identification and placement difficult. The fragments assembled on this plate are from at least twelve different manuscripts, including 4QpapIsa^b, fragment b, located at the far left side, third fragment from the bottom (Isa. 5:29-30).

Photo 6: Jumble of fragments on parchment. The fragments remain unidentified.

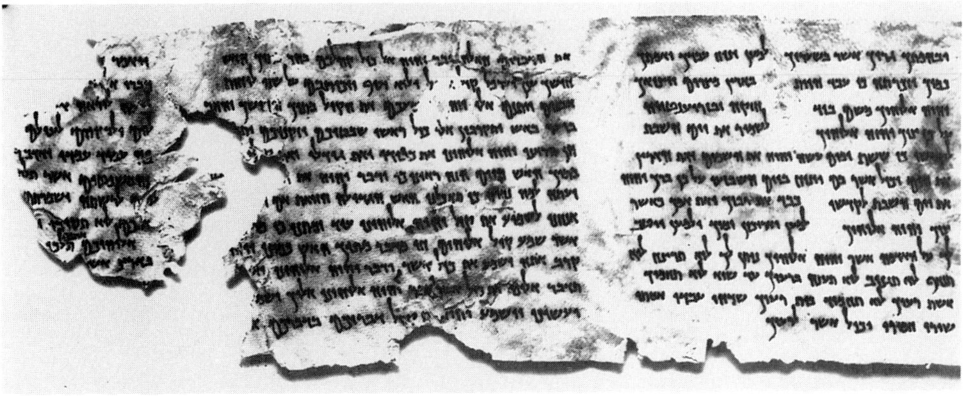

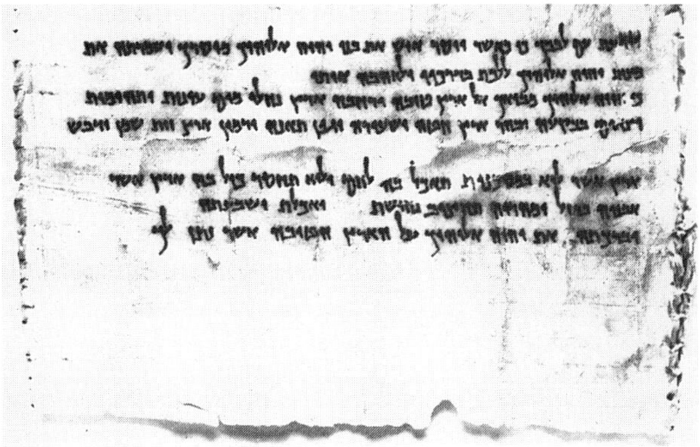

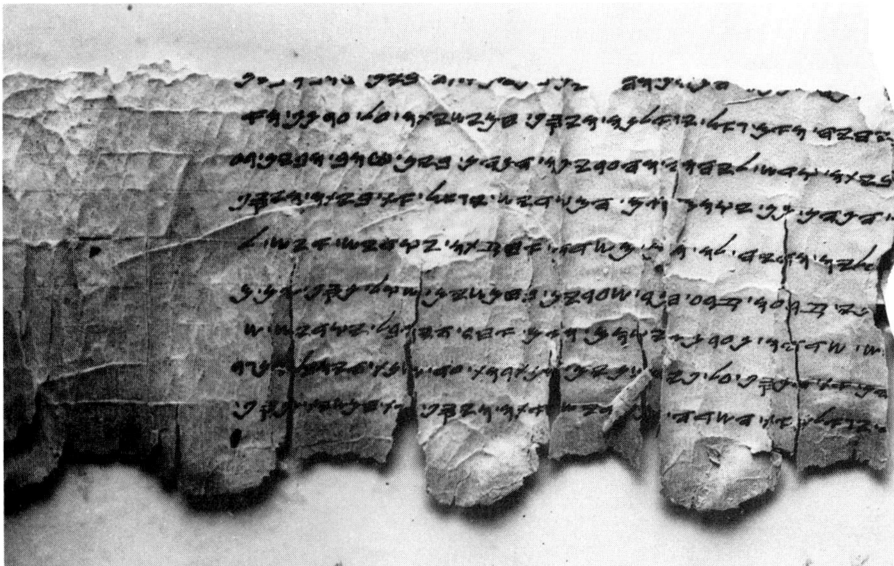

Photo 7 (above and left): 4QDeut^n. The column at the bottom of the photograph was originally attached to the right end of the main portion of the scroll in which all or parts of five columns survive. The text of the first column is Deuteronomy 8:5-10; the remaining columns contain Deuteronomy 5:1–6:1. Because the text is not in the sequence of the canonical book of Deuteronomy and the text contains harmonizing variants, White (1990a, 1990b) concluded that this is an "excerpted text."

Photo 8 (below): 11QpaleoLev, column 6, Leviticus 27:11-19. The left half of column 5 is seen on the right side of the photograph. The temporary join of columns 5 and 6 is visible. In Freedman and Mathews (1985:plate 10) the join has been repaired.

Photo 9 (above): QSam^a, fragments containing parts of 1 Samuel 1:22–2:24. This manuscript contains many variants that have been followed by the translators of the NAB and NRSV.

Photo 10 (right): 8Qmez: a mezuzah (an amulet hung on a doorpost), measuring only about 2½" by 7½", containing the text of Deuteronomy 10:12–11:21. The passage begins with the first great commandment, "Serve the Lord your God with all your heart and with all your soul," and contains a summary of the Lord's commandments. As instructed by Deuteronomy 11:20, "You shall write them upon the doorposts [*mezuzot*] of your house."

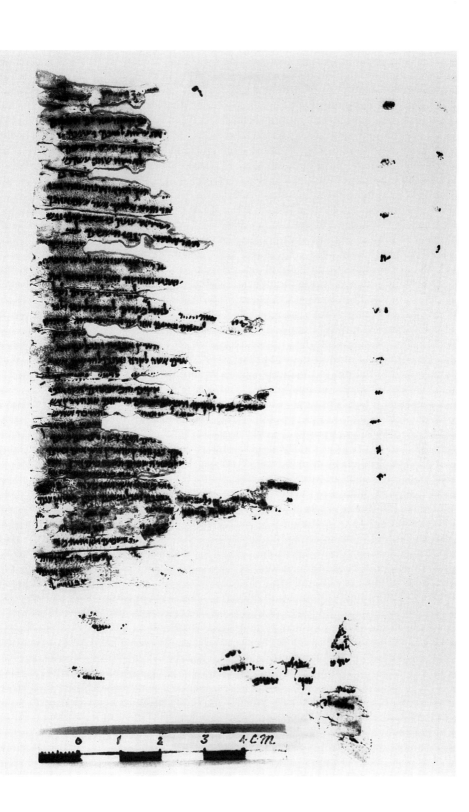

Photo 11 (top): 8Hev grXII, lower part of column 17, containing Habakkuk 2:4-8 (and the lower left-hand corner of column 18, 2:18-20). This Greek Minor Prophets scroll was found at Nahal Hever, about twenty-five miles south of Qumran. The translation seems to have been revised to bring the text closer to the Hebrew text.

Photo 12 (bottom): (2)Mur XII (= Mur88), column xix, Habakkuk 1:3–2:11 (and part of column xx). This Minor Prophets manuscript was found at Murabba'at, which is about eleven miles south of Qumran. The text is quite close to the Masoretic Text.

931231B   19.95 (13.95)